PERSO

Ellen Y. Siegelman, Ph.D., is a psychologist in the private practice of psychotherapy in San Francisco and Berkeley, California. Dr. Siegelman is associate clinical professor of medical psychology, Department of Psychiatry, University of California, San Francisco. The author of numerous articles based on her research on personality development and on the psychotherapy process, she is currently working on a book about the relationship between literature and psychology.

PERSONAL RISK

Mastering Change in Love and Work

Ellen Y. Siegelman

HARPER & ROW, PUBLISHERS, New York
Cambridge, Philadelphia, San Francisco,
London, Mexico City, São Paulo, Sydney

1817

Sponsoring Editor: Fred Henry
Project Coordinator: Total Concept Associates
Production Manager: Jeanie Berke
Compositor: Jay's Publisher's Services, Inc.
Printer and Binder: R. R. Donnelley & Sons Company

Personal Risk: Mastering Change in Love and Work

Copyright © 1983 by Harper & Row, Publishers, Inc.

Library of Congress Cataloging in Publication Data

Siegelman, Ellen.
  Personal risk.

  Bibliography: p.
  Includes index.
  1. Risk-taking (Psychology)   2. Change (Psychology)
3. Love.   4. Work—Psychological aspects. I. Title.
BF637.R57S54   1983   158'.2   82-21208
ISBN 0-06-046136-5

TO PHILIP, PETER, AND STEPHEN

Contents

Preface

This is a book for everyone who has ever made or is contemplating making a major life change: leaving home, getting married, starting or ending a deep relationship, deciding to have a child, choosing or changing a field of work. These are all major choice points that carry the possibilities of important gains and losses and that force us to step out of the well-worn grooves of our lives as we confront ourselves in basic ways. They offer the chance either of an expanded or diminished sense of self, of growth or stagnation, of hope or despair.

"Risk taking," a young friend of mine told me, "brings you face-to-face with your soul." It's a mirror of yourself. Along the path of risk, you fear you will see your true image and find out not only what you can do but what you can't. But sitting still, becoming paralyzed in the quicksand of fear, brings dangers too; staying put often leads to depression. And although moving on brings anxiety, the possibilities of exhilarating redefinition are enormous for those who can move on.

That is what this book is about: the terrors and the glories of taking risks—and how to minimize the terrors and enhance the glories.

I have written *Personal Risk* for the large number of curious and reflective people who want to take risks but are afraid to, in a time when more and more of us are choosing or being forced to make large-scale life changes. In this book, as in my work as a therapist, researcher, and teacher, I will focus on reducing the risk in risk taking so that the reader can be helped to go forward—sometimes stumblingly but, with increasing practice, more often resolutely.

Because practice is important, and because we have evidence that risk-taking skills are transferable from one situation to another, I have deliberately drawn my illustrations from a variety of risks—not from just one kind. This book is therefore different from the single-topic books that already exist in abundance—books on divorce, on career change, on childrearing. I will emphasize the characteristics common to many kinds of personal risk, so that although you may apply the principles and techniques to a current venture, you will also have a model that will be useful in mastering future challenges.

The problem of risky life change has absorbed me for more than two decades. I have been concerned personally, through two major moves and two career changes—from writer-editor to research psychologist and then to clinical psychologist. Professionally, I have come to think of my clinical work more and more as helping people to make significant life decisions when they find themselves frightened and sometimes even paralyzed. As both a researcher and a therapist, I have sought to discover what makes it possible for people to overcome their fear of doing what is most difficult for them.

In my work with people who suffer from severe constriction of the risk-taking ability (those who must take risks compulsively and those who avoid all risks), I have learned some important things that apply to people in the midrange—those of us who have some freedom of choice about which risks we will take and which we will defer. Work with less constricted patients and with people who are not in therapy has sharpened my understanding of the process that takes place when people approach with fear and excitement a dangerous life choice, such as getting married or divorced, leaving the religious life for the secular one, giving up financial security to take time out to think through their life course, leaving a particular field of work for a new, untried enterprise.

The ability to invite change—to take a personal risk—is a skill most of us need help with. But once people are able to do this dependably, their sense of selfhood blossoms, and their feeling that they are *living* their lives, not merely enduring or adapting, flourishes. The purpose of this book is to share the understanding born of my experience as a clinician, researcher, consultant, and teacher.

Understanding is the key operation. This is not a how-to-do-it book in the usual sense of that term. It does not contain page after page of exercises and quizzes—only a few crucial ones. It is, rather, a how-to-think-about-it book. I believe, with the Greeks, that right thinking leads us to right action and, with Freud, that thinking is indeed a kind of experimental action. My work as a therapist has convinced me again and again that the messages we give ourselves, the constructions we put on the important experiences of our lives, strongly shape what we will feel and what we will then do. The important underlying questions thus become: How can I understand both the risk-taking process and my own style and temperament? How can I work out a good match between them? As we shall see, risking a major change is always stressful, but through understanding, it can be made easier. Thus, instead of fleeing from risk or dashing blindly toward it, we can approach it welcomingly and can grow from it.

My conviction of the centrality of this subject has led me to write this book. In it, through case material, interviews, and research findings—my own and others'—I will explore a number of questions related to risky life changes: What is a risk? What misconceptions do people have about risks? What is the relationship between risk and change? Is there a risk in *not* risking? Are there different styles of risk taking? Do successful risk takers follow a specific process, and, if so, what is it? I will provide answers that I and others have found useful.

THE PLAN OF THE BOOK

In Chapter 1, I begin with a definition of personal risk and make some distinctions between kinds of risk (extended versus limited, chosen versus imposed), with anecdotal examples. I then turn to the question of what is seen as risky and what determines that perception.

In Chapter 2, we step back a bit to widen the focus and look at risk in the larger context of change, being particularly concerned with the costs as well as the benefits of change, the relation between life change and stress, and the establishment of a model for change-within-limits that will underlie the rest of the book.

The notion of differences in risk-taking style forms the theme of Chapter 3, in which a self-assessment questionnaire is followed by a description of the risk-taking styles that the reader can use for self-comparison.

Chapters 4 and 5 trace the courses of significant life changes made by people who are essentially fairly balanced risk takers, with different seasonings of impulsivity or cautiousness. Through extended case studies, we see six men and women taking risks that have become the prototypical major decisions of our time: having a child in one's thirties or getting a midlife divorce (Chapter 4), moving across the country and changing careers—either through quitting or being laid off (Chapter 5). I focus not only on the main issues in each of these risks but also on the various risk-taking *patterns* of these people: their relative planfulness, directness of approach, experienced difficulty, attempts to deal with losses, and self-evaluation.

In Chapter 6, I examine more extreme modes of risk taking in two people who have oversimplified decision rules that prevent the risk-taking process to develop *as a process*. These examples are used to highlight more typical issues we all face in initiating a major change: the fear of success and aggression, the fear of failure and weakness. This chapter is followed by an exercise designed to get the reader to introspect about the experience of having taken a major risk.

In Chapter 7, "Risk and the Sense of Self," I explore these psychological questions further, using my own research data to examine two of the central issues in risk taking: the deterrent of fear and the propellant of mastery. An attempt is made to reframe the definition of failure and to suggest ways of dealing with the fear of failure.

The final chapter, "Stages in the Risk-taking Process," puts the psychological insights, research findings, and anecdotal histories into a practical context. In spelling out the crucial components of undertaking a personal risk, I emphasize the importance of acknowledging ambivalence and the external and internal ways to reduce the risk of risk. We will see how such experience constitutes the potter's wheel on which we shape our sense of our limits and our possibilities. Following the final chapter is a "fantasy risk" exercise that enables readers to apply directly in their own lives the lessons learned in this book.

ACKNOWLEDGMENTS

I know much more about risk taking—particularly the risks of exposure and criticism—after having written this book than I did beforehand. I was lucky to have the support and counsel of friends, family, and colleagues.

Foremost among those who helped shape this book is Mitzi McClosky, a dear friend and respected colleague, who first encouraged me to speculate about the problems of risk taking and life change, to talk about it in courses and conferences, and finally to write about it. Her wisdom and encouragement at every step were indispensable.

I want to thank Jesse Miller, who offered just the right kind of support— uncritical—during the germinative stages of the book, and who kept me out of the library and at the writing desk.

Vivian Sutcher thoughtfully read the manuscript and made useful suggestions in her role as consulting editor for Harper & Row.

Barbara Wolfinger read the manuscript closely and generously offered her special blend of ingenuity and practicality all along the way.

Other friends and colleagues who read the entire manuscript in various versions and gave me the benefit of their constructive suggestions were: Carol Calvert, Constance Crawford, Mary Ruggieri, Stephen Siegelman, Bernard Weiner, and Carol Wildavsky.

Portions of the book were read and useful comments were made by my six psychologist friends who have met as a group since 1975, and by Herbert McClosky.

Finally, I want to acknowledge the contribution of the people I interviewed, who talked about their own major transitions and graciously allowed me to use their stories (with appropriate safeguards for confidentiality). And I must also thank my patients, who have taught me most of what I know about risk taking—what it is that blocks people and what it takes to set them free to risk.

My debt to all these people—and to the members of my family, who sustained and encouraged me—is enormous.

Ellen Y. Siegelman

PERSONAL RISK

Part I
SETTING THE STAGE

Chapter 1
What Is Personal Risk
and Why Is It Important?

> We can never be really prepared for that which is wholly
> new. We have to adjust ourselves, and every radical ad-
> justment is a crisis in self-esteem: we undergo a test, we
> have to prove ourselves. It needs inordinate self-
> confidence to face drastic change without inner trembling.
>
> Eric Hoffer, *The Ordeal of Change*

The middle-aged man I am interviewing stands up and begins pacing and gesturing animatedly as he talks about his career change from lawyer to real estate salesman. The young woman I am seeing in treatment leans forward in her chair and unself-consciously places her hand on her heart as she describes her fear and pleasure in starting a new relationship. The graduate student in literature tells me with anguish that he is blocked in writing his dissertation and feels immobilized and scared. And a teacher thinking of changing fields writes: "I know it's not just a job I'm looking for, it's my own self, which means that my whole life is at stake and in my hands."

What these people are talking about in one way or another—in word, gesture, the flash of an eye, the tilt of the head—is a highly charged topic for them: the challenge or life change that represents a personal risk. These changes are important because they help us define who we are and what we may become—in short, our basic sense of self.

When I talk about the self in this context I do not mean the narcissistic self we have heard so much about of late: looking out for "Number 1," "winning," self-gratification, self-encapsulation. I am thinking, rather, of the basic feeling of "what it is to be me" that we observe when we become self-conscious, self-critical, or self-affirming. No matter how great our communion with or concern for others, our sense of self is what we live and die with. Taking a big risk means putting that self totally on the line. How we manage this crucial transaction determines whether "good-self" or "bad-self" feelings triumph.

Most of us struggle for most of our lives, consciously or unconsciously, trying to become humane and compassionate to that self, trying to recognize its true power and accept its real limitations. In my work as a therapist, I strive to help people in their efforts to become more realistic about that self, to give up equally distorted notions of omnipotence and of impotence as they learn to disclaim responsibility for what is ultimately outside their control (childhood traumas, their parents' life histories), and to claim responsibility for what they have done to perpetuate their own suffering. As psychologist Roy Schafer puts it, a major goal of therapy is that the patient (client, analysand) "progressively recognizes, accepts, refines, and lives in terms of the idea of *the self as agent.*"

Risk taking offers the opportunity for similar kinds of growth, for similar experiences of the self as agent in the natural setting. In that setting, the growth can be called mastery or a kind of self-therapy. In risk taking, the ultimate questions we grapple with are these profound questions about "who I am": To what extent can I direct my own life? How much must I yield to the world around me, and how much can I shape that world in my own terms? What will I think about myself if I stay where I am, refusing this risk? What will I think about myself if I try this dangerous enterprise and fail? What if I try and succeed—could there be costs attached to that too? Why is change so hard, even when it's something I seem to want? How can it be made easier and more rewarding?

Our first steps are to get a map of the terrain—to define what personal risk is and what sets it apart from risk in general; to sketch out some distinctions among kinds of personal risk—limited versus extended, chosen versus imposed—with examples and illustrations; and finally to look at which enterprises people consider personally risky and what determines their perception. Because my approach is psychological, I will emphasize throughout the importance of the *meanings* such experiences have for individuals.

TOWARD A DEFINITION OF PERSONAL RISK

Webster tells us risk is "hazard, peril, exposure to loss or injury." This global and general definition looks at risk from the outside and suggests the actuarial risks that are so crucial to insurance companies, planners, and policy makers. These are the people who compute the odds of your getting lung cancer by age 55 if you're a three-pack-a-day smoker, the risk of hitting a car if you drive while drunk, the risk of getting coronary disease if you have a family history of heart trouble and a high lipid count, and so on.

Important as such calculations and judgments may be, these are not the kinds of issues that concern us here. Instead of looking at risk from the outside, we will be looking at risk from *inside*—from the point of view of the person assessing the danger.

A major life change—getting married, getting divorced, having a child late in life, "coming out" as a homosexual, changing a career, moving across the

country—is subjectively experienced as an uncertain and dangerous enterprise, offering possibilities of significant losses as well as gains. Such situations
produce what Robert Abelson has called "hot cognitions"—thoughts about
vital, affect-laden problems, as opposed to the "cool cognitions" of routine
problem solving. Hot cognitions are fueled by the need to make highly
conflictual decisions that commit us to a course of action that carries long-term
consequences. In talking of personal risk, then, in addition to change and
danger, we must introduce the subjective element of *conflict*—the conflict
between comfortable but often deadening security and frightening but also
exhilarating change. Conflict and ambivalence are hallmarks of risk that will
concern us in the remainder of this book.

We can characterize the personal risk represented by major life change by
these important elements:

1. uncertainty about outcome, with an inability to assess the odds
   precisely
2. the possibility of significant *losses* as well as gains
3. permanence of consequences—effects that are long-term and possibly
   irreversible
4. a high degree of personal significance—the sense that the undertaking
   calls upon a central part of the self or forces one *to define or redefine
   oneself* in very basic ways.

Although the first two elements are included in the general or dictionary
definition of risk, it is the last two—particularly the high degree of personal
significance—that I want to emphasize in talking about personal risk.

The Personally Significant Risk

No one else can define for you what *you* experience as dangerous. Although
there is general agreement that major life change is fraught with danger, any
one person may not experience a given change in that way. What is a matter of
course to one person may be agony to another. At the end of this chapter, we
will look at what accounts for some of these differences. The subjectively
riskiest choices—those in which you put your whole self on the line—will vary
tremendously from person to person. The following examples (with names and
other identifying details changed, as in all the examples in this book) will
illustrate the point:

Mark, a somewhat introverted 34-year-old sculptor, suddenly found that he
was unable to sculpt, after a brief period when he had been very prolific. He
turned away from his sculpture for a while, choosing to become a real estate
salesman, which was difficult because it called on him to be more assertive and
persuasive and to deal more directly with people than he would have wished.
Nevertheless, he found the work far less stressful—and risky—than sculpting.

"If I fail at this," he told me, "it's no big deal, because it doesn't mean that much to me. It's not *who I am*. But if I go back to sculpture and fail, I'll be utterly demoralized."

Similarly, Gregory, a history professor, can joke about his ineptitude at balancing his checkbook because being a successful manager of his own finances is not essential to his self-esteem. But he agonizes over every word he writes, checking and rechecking the thesaurus, sketching out four alternatives for every phrase. His writing is highly invested; it opens up the risks of exposure and criticism that could be devastating to his sense of self.

Hot Cognitions and Cool Models

In all significant, chancy enterprises that entail profound consequences, we may try to follow the rational models that economists and decision theorists have proposed, but we can never do this mechanically or straightforwardly. Most of these models call for a rational scanning of alternatives and a calculation of probable gains and losses. Although rationality in decision making is to be prized and striven for, we must also realize its limitations. These limitations stem from imperfect information, human impatience, and the difficulty of adding into our equations the emotional components of hope and fear, not to mention our unconscious projections and fantasies.

These limitations of quantitative or computer models for decision making are also reflected in research on risk taking, which, for all its rigor, can be only suggestive. To the extent that laboratory research gives us exact results, it often does so at the expense of breadth or relationship to real life. There is, by now, a fairly extensive research literature on risk taking,* but most of it raises the specter that all laboratory studies raise: What is important is difficult to measure; what can be measured precisely is often trivial.

In most of the risk-taking research, either no costs are involved or the costs are relatively slight—especially when compared to the costs entailed in a major life decision such as marrying, divorcing, or making a major job change or a geographical move. People may appear to behave like computer models of rational decision making when the consequences of their choices are relatively minor—that is, when they are dealing with "cool cognitions." But such models can rarely be approximated under stress. We will need to recognize and cope

---

*The research done by psychologists has been mainly on two basic types of risk taking: hypothetical choice dilemmas and actual gambling wagers. For the first type, the subject is given a decision problem to solve; for example, "Mr. X., a computer programmer, has the option of staying with his present job at a satisfactory but modest salary or of moving to another position that will pay him higher wages but offers no long-term security." The respondent is asked to indicate what odds of success (ranging from 1 in 10 through 9 in 10) he or she would require in order to choose the riskier alternative. In the wager situations, subjects are asked to gamble at different odds, with the possibility of actually gaining or losing small sums of money.

with this fact of emotional life rather than imposing a highly formal model that has very little to do with how people actually behave. That is why I shall acknowledge the findings of research where they seem useful but will rely more heavily on clinical data, personal interviews, and other material drawn from life situations.

FURTHER DISTINCTIONS: LIMITED VERSUS EXTENDED RISKS, CHOSEN VERSUS IMPOSED RISKS

In addition to being characterized by uncertainty and the possibility of losses, personal risk is distinguished by having long-lasting consequences and a high degree of personal significance. Among the risks that embody these criteria, we can make some further useful distinctions: Are the risks limited or extended? Are they chosen or imposed? Being able to talk in these terms will help us account for the flavor or "feel" of certain personal risks.

Limited versus Extended Risks

Most of the risks we will be considering represent major life shifts—marriages, separations, work discontinuities, geographical moves. These can be described as ramified or *extended* risks—extended in time and in psychological space. The space they cut across deeply is your life space—your world as defined by your literal, physical self and its extensions through thought and action to other people and institutions. Put more simply, when you change your career, you change not only your perception of yourself but also the texture of your days, the people you work with, even your time away from work (particularly if the job is demanding and absorbing). Your feelings about the job will influence your relationships with your spouse or children, your friends, your colleagues. Moreover, the change goes on affecting you and them for an indefinite time in most phases of your life. Because this kind of risk is often irreversible—or is reversible only with very painful consequences—you make a formidable commitment in making such a move.

What about an encapsulated or *limited* risk? This type of change is limited either in time or in the amount of your life it preempts, or both. A limited risk has a more clearly defined beginning and end point. Although it may and often does send large ripples through the rest of our lives, we perceive it as basically contained. It is not a major change involving work or love, but it may arise from a specific problem area and may call on specific skills and talents. Examples of such risks are learning to water-ski if you've always lived in Kansas and are afraid of the water, traveling alone for the first time, taking full responsibility for directing a membership campaign for a civic organization, and—the limited risk that most people are most afraid of—speaking in public.

These ventures often entail doing a fearful thing for the first time—stepping out into an alien space and annexing it to the territory of yourself. In

George Orwell's *1984*, the room in which each prisoner was put to confront his or her terror was called Room 101. Being diabolically astute, the agents of Big Brother saw to it that the contents of Room 101 were exquisitely tailored to the deepest secret fears of each prisoner who entered it—it contained "the worst thing in the world" for that particular person. Winston Smith, the hero of *1984*, was morbidly afraid of rats; for him, Room 101 was filled with these scurrying, squealing rodents.

Breaking into your personal Room 101, however briefly and tentatively, has highly important consequences for your sense of self and hence for the rest of your life. In every case, you are confronting some central dread, if only in a limited way.

Let's look at some examples of limited risks and spell out the central fear that is being faced in each case:

TRAVELING ALONE

Susan, a secretary in her late twenties, writes: A recent major risk was to take this past summer off and travel in Europe by myself. I had never traveled alone before, and the only country I had ever visited outside the U.S. was Canada. Approximately six months before I actually left I had planned to make this trip. I was very excited about my decision and very scared. I had lots of anxious feelings about not being able to get a hotel room, order meals, buy tickets, make friends, generally get around in countries where I did not speak the language. In anticipation of my trip I read several "how to travel" books and general books about the countries I would be visiting. I talked to friends who had traveled, especially those who had traveled by themselves on limited budgets. I made lists of places they recommended, and got lots of good advice on hosteling, *pensions*, and addresses of friends and relatives in Europe that I could call on. I also took a course on "Traveling and the Single Woman" offered through a local adult education program.

I did at last get on the plane, and off I went to Europe. Overall, I had a wonderful time. I quickly learned the ins and outs of getting inexpensive places to stay and ways of traveling with discounts. Advice from friends really paid off. I found it quite easy to meet other travelers, and I also met "natives." The big fear—eating alone—didn't happen nearly as often as I expected. I traveled for three months without any major traumas.

As a result, I felt very good about myself for initiating, planning, and carrying out my trip. I felt that I had been self-reliant and that I could make good decisions for myself. I learned to figure out what I really wanted to do and how to implement it. I would not hesitate to travel again on my own. I was glad that I had given myself all the little "crutches"—the course, books, friends' advice. They helped make me a more independent person.

The underlying psychological issue that this limited risk addressed was Susan's fear of not being able to cope when her usual supports were absent, of feeling isolated and panicky, and of feeling "like a helpless woman."

PUBLIC SPEAKING: A FIRST-TIME TV APPEARANCE

Risks that have to do with performing or speaking in public—exposing oneself to public criticism and possible humiliation—are frequently mentioned. Marion, a legislative aide in her mid-thirties, describes her first television appearance:

> Recently I was asked to be on a TV show to speak on an issue that vitally affected education. I'd never before been on TV except once when a candid cameraman was asking passersby how they planned to celebrate Christmas. What I had at stake was my image, and whether or not I'd make a complete fool of myself.
>
> I was ambivalent about accepting the challenge—on the one hand, I was fearful, anxious, etc. At the same time I was curious about how I'd come across and whether I'd be effective in communicating ideas. It was like there were two parts of me: one scared stiff, and the other somewhat detached and looking on. And maybe a third part—the hidden "star" who leaped at the opportunity to be a "celebrity."
>
> I accepted the risk, having decided that if it went contrary to my expectations I could use the defense I had created for myself: "Well, the issue—the proposed legislation—was worth speaking out against, even if I did not do an outstanding job." Despite my fear, the television segment went well, I received good feedback from people who had seen the program, and I did not have to fall back on any prepared defense.
>
> After this episode I gained more confidence in myself and my abilities. I'm more willing now to project myself publicly when it comes to expressing opinions and views on current issues—even at the risk of making a fool of myself.

The central dread that Marion confronted in taking this risk was the possibility of incurring shame and humiliation.

A MIDLIFE JOURNEY

A different kind of issue is faced in the next risk, described to me by a middle-aged man whom I'll call George. Having taught for almost twenty years, George had begun to feel that his life had settled into an unbearable rut: a safe, dull marriage and a safe, dull job. He felt that his life should demand more from him and give more to him than this. Indeed, from young adulthood on he had been driven by the idea of a quest or a test. He wasn't about to trek through the Himalayas, and hang-gliding wasn't his style. For several years he pondered the kind of test he would seek. What would it be like to tackle the unknown head on? To guarantee that new and unexpected things would happen? To push his ingenuity and resourcefulness to their limits? To introduce some noise into the deadly quiet of his life?

At age 45, George decided to take a 30-day, 3,000-mile hitchhiking trip around the southwestern United States, with only a small day pack and a sleeping bag—in effect, to become a hobo for a month.

When he told his wife about his plan, she was very upset and told him that it was a crazy idea and that she couldn't understand what on earth was driving him to do something so melodramatic and self-punishing. (Their marriage, he told me, has subsequently broken up.) George was undeterrable; he promised her he would drop her a postcard every day so that she would know he was all right.

George set out with only ten dollars in cash, taking a credit card as a fail-safe but promising himself not to use it except in dire emergencies. He also pledged to himself to return with ten dollars in his pocket—getting odd jobs to support himself so that his journey would end up costing him nothing. It was a kind of game he was playing with himself. He approached the trip with "apprehensive exhilaration." For him, the central question was his fear of the unknown and a lingering suspicion that he might be tempting fate by playing this kind of game with life. He did have the reassurance that the risk would be time-limited, however, and he did as much advance planning as he could. In his words:

> I planned carefully what I would take and where I would go—then I left the rest up to my ingenuity in coping with situations as they arose. I slept by the roadside, in fields and sand dunes—and in motels when I had earned some money. I hitched rides with 54 people in all—some drunk, some gay, some old, some young, some rich, some poor—an evangelist, a man just out of prison for assault and battery, one woman, several truck drivers. . . . I rode the rails on a freight train and traveled a stretch by plane after I had earned the fare.
>
> The outcome? I survived. I was more than 20 pounds lighter, and I had some incredible experiences, many of them scary. I was very proud that I undertook this journey of adventure and discovery, a journey that was as much a discovery of myself as of the places I passed through. This was a high point in my life and now, seven years later, I'm trying to think what I can do in *this* decade that will again shake up my life and help me once again test my limits.

Because risks of this kind require us to face down our fears, they can make us feel more powerful if we master them. For this reason, they are good practice for the major life choices and changes we must all make in the course of our lives. The residue left behind from such a limited risk, if successful, is the feeling "I did it! I actually made myself do something hard and frightening. And the next time I face such a challenge—or any challenge—it should be easier." In short, these limited risks help us see ourselves as being able to create desired change.

But what if we fail? The whole question of "failure" in one of these ventures is moot. It depends very much on what we choose to evaluate. Suppose the young woman who traveled to Europe had had a less enjoyable trip than she did. Suppose, instead of success upon success, she'd had a number of the usual travel disasters sprinkled in. Would her trip—and her risk—then have been a failure? Not necessarily—not if she had chosen to think of success or failure as applied to the willingness to extend herself, *to the choice and the process, rather than to the final outcome or end point.*

Evaluation of risk need not depend only on what actually happened—the external or real-world outcome. It can also depend very much on how we feel about ourselves as risk takers. A friend of mine, deploring the absence of rites of passage in our culture, praised the Jewish Bar Mitzvah ceremony as one of the few such rites, adding, "And you know, the wonderful thing is you can't flunk a Bar Mitzvah!" This does not mean that some 13-year-olds don't do better and some worse in their reading of their portion of the Torah and commentary, but only that the *attempt* is what counts.

Chosen versus Imposed Risks

In addition to categorizing risks as primarily limited or primarily extended, we can differentiate among them on the basis of how much choice the individual appears to have in confronting the danger situation.

Here are some examples of imposed risks:

Beth had been married for 15 years to Jonathan, a moderately successful lawyer. They had two adolescent sons. For years their marriage had been rocky: she would nag and he would retreat into silence. But they shared many interests—gardening, home improvement, backpacking, theater—and they were devoted parents. Sexually, they had been estranged for some time, but Beth was not acutely depressed about that. She enjoyed her part-time work as a reporter for a local weekly and her volunteer activities as a Big Sister. She took great pleasure in her children, and she and Jonathan had periods of relative compatibility, particularly on vacations. She did not expect or even very much want anything to change.

One day Jonathan came home from work and, without any warning, blurted out, "I can't sit on this any longer, Beth. I don't love you any more. I haven't for years, but I made do for the kids. Now I've met someone I care about very much, and we want to live together. I'm leaving on Saturday."

Howard, a computer analyst, was persuaded by an executive recruiter to leave his job in Detroit and move to a computer firm in Manhattan, uprooting his wife Ann, a biologist, and his four children. Ann was willing to relocate because opportunities for finding work in her field were good and because the move meant much more money for the family and a desirable location for all of them. (Both Ann and Howard had grown up in New York City and had always felt it was their real home.) Within a year, through circumstances no one could have foreseen, Howard found himself out of a job because the development of a highly advanced system by a rival firm had caused his company to go into bankruptcy. He was given a half-year's severance pay and was told regretfully to look for another job.

These two situations—being divorced and being laid off—bring tremendous risks with them, risks that are not of the person's choosing but are imposed by the actions of others, close or distant, known or unknown. (In another category of imposed risks—natural disasters—the hazards are imposed by forces outside human control.)

Imposed risks share some common characteristics:

1. They are almost always experienced as negative—carrying immediately and overwhelmingly unfavorable consequences.
2. They typically contain an element of surprise or unpredictability and are perceived as occurring at the wish or even, in some cases, at the whim of others.
3. They therefore evoke immediate feelings of helplessness, of being out of control, of being victimized.
4. They sound the knell of loss—loss of a mate, loss of a job, and the loss of self-esteem that frequently accompanies these losses. For this reason, they qualify as major stressors.

One response to such stressors is to give in or give up. Another course is to try to salvage what we can from a painful situation, to "make the best of a bad bargain." This is essentially viewed as a deficit operation. We talk about "making do" or "coping" in such cases; and although we value coping, the term nevertheless has a reactive, adaptive flavor.

When we do manage to affirm our sense of self in the face of imposed risk, we come to feel that we can take what life dishes out. Initially, at least (and this may change as we become more adept at turning disasters into opportunities), the metaphor for our response is a holding operation: battening down the hatches, holding our ground, staying afloat, keeping our head above water, surviving.

These reactive, coping skills lead to accommodation, or what used to be called adjustment—forcing ourselves to fit the molds the world has thrust upon us. Perhaps the best we can hope for in the case of imposed risk is to be able to say, "I have been tested and have passed the test." This may be no small satisfaction, but if it were all any of us were capable of, we would be stuck with a limited idea of our possibilities, seeing ourselves, at best, only as stoic endurers. For many people in the world whose choices unfortunately are limited by poverty, lack of education, or illness, such coping or hanging on may indeed be the best they can hope for. Nevertheless, as we shall see later, most of us have some leeway in perceiving a given risk as chosen or imposed.

What about a chosen risk—what might that look like?

A CHOSEN RISK FOR AN ADOPTED DAUGHTER

Marianne, now a Milwaukee account executive in her mid-forties, had grown up as an adopted child in a middle-class family on the East Coast. She had learned at age 7 that she was adopted, as was her 12-year-old "sister." Later, her adoptive parents confirmed that she had been adopted at 18 months and had lived with her original mother until then. Even before she knew that fact,

Marianne had felt, she now says retrospectively, that she didn't belong in that family. Her adoptive mother, a decent and well-intentioned but emotionally cool woman, had had trouble handling Marianne, who was more willful and tempestuous than her docile older sister.

For years Marianne wondered about her real parents. When things were rough at home or at school, she would console herself with the idea that she was a "gypsy princess." The fantasy sounded romantic and made her feel special and interesting. But many years later—when she was in her late thirties—she took a trip through Spain and saw real gypsies living in caves in incredible poverty and squalor. One of them, in fact, ran up to her and offered to sell her a baby. Her heart froze, and she knew she could never invoke that fantasy again. She continued to feel uncertain and confused. The question that had troubled her all her life—"Who am I *really?*"—became more and more pressing.

Three and a half years ago, when she was 41, Marianne's adoptive father died, and her adoptive mother gave her the original adoption papers. She saw her name, Carol Sue K——— (disguised here, of course), and the name of her birth mother. She knew for the first time in her life that, if she wanted to, she could try to track down her mother. But she was put off because, some years before, a lawyer friend had told her that, if she were to pursue the search, she might uncover deeply upsetting facts: she could have been born in prison or born to someone who was seriously disturbed.

She thought some more about it and read an article in a women's magazine outlining the perils and rewards experienced by women who had tracked down their mothers. Finally, she decided to start the hunt, feeling that she could always choose *not* to act on any information she got. She settled on a private investigator, who assured her absolutely that her birth mother would not know that the investigation was taking place. Then she waited. Six months later, the investigator presented her with a formidable bill and a six-page report outlining all the facts known about her birth mother: she had married someone other than Marianne's father, she had had a large family, and she was living in straitened circumstances in a state not far from where Marianne was born. The report also gave her address and her phone number.

As Marianne sat looking at that number, with its long-distance area code, she began—just as an exercise—to sketch out a scenario of what she might say if she called this woman. She read through the scenario she had written, and she felt terrified. What if the woman rejected her? What if she, Marianne, caused her birth mother to become so upset that she became ill? What if she found out something awful in the process? On the other hand, what if she was welcomed and could put this huge missing part into the picture puzzle of her life? She still had 20 minutes until she had to leave for work.

"Somehow," she says, "I found my hand reaching out and dialing the number." A woman's voice answered on the other end.

"Mrs. K———?" Marianne asked.

"Yes, who is this?" A steady voice, a bit wary.

Marianne went into her script:

"I'm someone you knew a long time ago. Forty-one years ago. My name then was Carol Sue K————."

There was silence, and then the woman said, "Oh, you must be my niece Annie's daughter.... "

Marianne repeated her "lines," and this time her birth mother recognized who she was. "My God," she cried, "I can't believe it."

They talked for 15 minutes. Marianne told her of her fears of upsetting her, and her mother said, with a laugh, "Did you expect to hear a loud thud from this end—that I'd keeled over?" Her mother told her that every year on Marianne's birthday—July 15—"I think about you and wonder where you are and who you turned out to be." She also told her that her present husband had never known of Marianne's birth 41 years ago. The two women promised to write each other.

Six months later, after several letters had been exchanged, the two women took the further risk of meeting. They arranged to meet in the Port of New York Authority terminal at a specific exit. As Marianne described it:

> I asked her, "How will I know you?" She just said, confidently, "You'll know me." And I did. There was this small, dumpy lady—with a bumpy nose just like mine. We looked, we hugged, we cried, and then we spent the day together talking, shopping, and going to a museum. I took her to lunch at a fancy restaurant, someplace where we wouldn't be hassled and could talk for a long time. She was a *little* uncomfortable; she's used to living very modestly and wasn't quite sure about which fork to use.

Marianne immediately saw things that delighted her in her birth mother—the same kind of pluck she herself has, a whimsical turn that Marianne describes as "fey," and a stubborn independence. Her mother loves to read, despite (or perhaps in some ways because of) her limited educational background.

Through her, Marianne learned of the circumstances of her birth and learned that her father had been a 19-year-old with whom her mother had had a brief affair. Her mother described going to another city, having her child, trying to keep her until it became financially impossible, and then having to put her up for adoption. "I did have a choice between the family you were sent to and a minister's family. Somehow," her mother grinned, "I just couldn't see you in a minister's family."

The two women continue to write regularly, and Marianne hopes her mother will come to visit her in Milwaukee one day. That may not happen until her mother's husband dies. Meanwhile, each continues to validate the other. Marianne sums it up:

> My mother sees that she made a good decision, and this has been a tremendous relief to her. And I have found myself accounted for—in some mysterious way "explained" by this woman who gave birth to me and tried to raise me until she

could no longer do so. I wouldn't recommend this search for every adopted person, and, God knows, it was very dangerous. So much could have gone wrong. But I'm the kind of person who prefers knowing—even knowing the worst—to uncertainty. I'm overwhelmingly glad I took this risk. It was the most dangerous and, I would have to say, the most positive thing I've ever done.

Risks that are chosen feel different from risks we experience as imposed. They require us to expose ourselves to anxiety deliberately, actually to *court* anxiety. They force us to take the chance of loss as well as gain. Unlike the imposed risk, whose metaphor was "holding on," the metaphor we attach to chosen risks is "moving ahead." Instead of a deficit operation, we operate out of a sense of abundance, as though we're upping the ante on our lives and our self-worth.

Furthermore, when we feel "I choose to challenge myself" rather than "I respond to what life deals me," we are moving the source of control of our lives inward. Thus the very act of challenging ourselves makes us feel autonomous. We are not merely adapting to the environment but are shaping it. We become actors, not spectators or victims. We mold the environment to us, rather than accommodating ourselves to it. With this thrust, we can choose the terror and dose it; it no longer has to come headlong at us unaware.

DECIDING TO PERCEIVE A RISK AS CHOSEN OR IMPOSED

Having underscored the distinction between imposed and chosen risks, I now want to blur or modify it somewhat. The constraints imposed by a situation often are actually ambiguous or mixed, and we can set our seal on the risk in the way we choose to *perceive* it. We can, for instance, take aspects of an imposed risk and convert them into opportunities for active choice and reorganization. Conversely, we can choose—and we often do this unconsciously—to see an opportunity for risk as a trap and a snare, as though we *had* no choice.

We all experience anxiety some of the time, but the difference between those who are more active and those who are more passive in handling stress is reflected in how they see the challenge. Some people always behave like good, compliant students, responding to the world as if it were imposing tests that they will pass or fail. Others see the world as somewhat responsive to their own activity; much of the time *they* impose the tasks and the tests. Psychologists talk about these two kinds of people as having relatively greater "external" or "internal" locus of control—a fancy way of saying that they systematically choose to view either external forces or internal forces as more powerful in shaping their behavior.

Although some risks are clearly imposed (the prototype is a natural disaster) and some are clearly volitional (choosing to change a career), *most challenges have elements of both choice and imposition; it is how we interpret them that makes all the difference.* We frequently have the chance to respond either as copers or as venturers. What we choose depends on our temperament, style, and life history.

Sarah is a 29-year-old weaver whose father had been extremely domineering and sometimes even sadistic. Sarah has chosen to interpret virtually every encounter with another person as exemplifying that model from her childhood. Thus she saw her husband as "forcing" her to continue her nonlucrative work because he felt it was "significant," when she had said she wanted to get a better paying but less prestigious sales job. Similarly, her therapist was "forcing" her to continue coming to therapy twice a week, when she had talked about reducing the frequency of her sessions with him. She felt victimized on all sides.

In fact, Sarah actually was comfortable with and even sought out the role of victim. Her perception of the other person (her husband, her therapist) as "forcing" her allowed her to play out that role. It also served other functions, including allowing her to express her own wishes without acknowledging them. She really wanted to continue working as a weaver, for example, but she did not feel justified in persisting. She also had some strong wishes *not* to reduce her commitment to therapy, but by converting the therapist into her tyrannical or arbitrary parent, she could reduce her ambivalence by perceiving the wish to continue as coming from him, while *she* acknowledged only her wish to disengage. For such a person, even a risk that has been chosen—in Sarah's case, pursuing a gratifying but financially unrewarding career—will often appear to be imposed. Eventually, Sarah came to recognize how much of her view was her own construction and how much freedom of choice she actually had.

I do not mean to suggest that we have the freedom to see our world as entirely of our own making. Indeed, such a perception represents the grandiose delusion of a psychotic, who believes he or she is responsible for national events or physical calamities. I want to emphasize, however, that many of the situations we encounter are truly mixed; among their many facets, some, at least, are highly amenable to our control.

We can see this in the following example:

Consuela, a bilingual teacher of Spanish-speaking children, learned that she was to be evaluated by a new principal. Although she had had nearly a dozen years of teaching experience, she very much dreaded being criticized, especially by this principal, whom she didn't much respect. While worrying about being observed the next day, she suddenly thought, "What would I *like* to do in the class tomorrow? And what could I do that would actually teach the principal something about what *I* think is important in working with bilingual kids?" In thinking this way, she was able to redefine or *reframe* the task and to change her position vis-à-vis the principal. She transformed herself in her own eyes from a submissive employee on trial to a colleague and even, in some sense, a superior ("What can I teach *him*?"). This refocusing helped her reduce her anxiety, so that she was able to bring some of her typical zest to her preparation and delivery. She thus changed an imposed risk into a chosen one and transmuted feelings of helplessness into feelings of efficacy.

An even more extreme example is our response to the death of someone very close to us. This life change is clearly an imposition, a stress not chosen. But in our handling of it, we have many chances to structure our responses in creative ways, so that, ultimately, we can feel that we are not only shaping our responses but shaping our very selves.

A young woman in her thirties, who told me she had always been terrified by thoughts of death, chose to be present during the last days of her mother's terminal illness, rather than staying where she was living (in another state), communicating only by phone or letter, and letting her father and sister handle her mother's dying until the very end.

This is how she describes the process:

> I was fearful of reexperiencing loss, fearful of the unknown—including how I was going to handle my feelings of helplessness and grief. I wanted to run from the situation but also wanted to be there—for myself and my parents.
>
> I made what may seem to some people like a too-deliberate or even schoolbook attempt to prepare myself, but then I've been a lifelong student, and one way I deal with change is by studying up on what I'm afraid of. So I read Elisabeth Kubler-Ross's book *On Death and Dying* and was even able to borrow tapes of a presentation that Dr. Kubler-Ross had given at the local university. Both of these really helped reduce my anxiety. I also recontacted my former therapist to help me get clear about what I really wanted to do and to explore my feelings.
>
> Then I went back home and tried to handle the uncompleted work of saying goodbye to my mother—to let her know what she had meant to me. I grieved with my sister, helped around the house to reduce the demands on my father. I visited the hospital frequently, even at the end when Mother was comatose, and I spent time with the close relatives who had come to see her.
>
> I helped plan the funeral arrangements, the memorial service, and the budget for the family. I went through it all, helping my father with details about the death certificate and the estate, and even spent two weeks going through the closets.
>
> It was painful and difficult, and I was in tears a lot of the time. But through it I experienced a sense of completion of my relationship with my mother and a working through of my grief, though I still miss her and often feel very sad when I think of her.
>
> As a result of having chosen to *engage* in this experience rather than watch from the sidelines, I felt proud of myself and responsible. I now find death much less frightening—my own and anyone else's—and I am truly glad that I did not avoid this incredible opportunity for personal growth.

This vignette reminds us that, although many limits are set by circumstances or, if you will, by fate, we still have considerable leeway for perceiving how much control we can exercise, how much we can use our fear as a stimulus to growth, and how much of ourselves we can ingeniously call on to leave our mark on what we do.

WHAT PEOPLE CONSIDER TO BE PERSONAL RISKS AND WHY

We turn now to people's actual experience—what people consider to be significant personal risks. For this purpose, I shall draw upon my own research on nearly 300 adults who were concerned with making major life changes. Although these risks may have some elements in common with the major life changes we will look at in considering stress in Chapter 2, I have chosen to focus on *invited* or *sought-out* challenges rather than on the imposed risks that bulk so large in the research on stressful life events. Because of my interest in people's efforts to extend themselves and to perceive themselves as agents of their destinies, I asked my research subjects to talk about *risks or challenges that they themselves had initiated.* It is interesting to see how these participants in workshops and courses on career change responded when they were asked to describe "a situation in your life in which you chose to face a major challenge or take an important risk."

By way of background, most of these people were educators—teachers, school counselors, or administrators—who were seeking or being forced to consider career alternatives to education. Other groups included middle managers who were trying to move ahead in their careers and a substantial number of liberal arts graduates of varied backgrounds who were eager to redefine their vocational goals. The workshops were given through the General Extension Division of the University of California, Berkeley, and the Career Placement Center of Stanford University.

The participants ranged in age from their mid-twenties to their mid-fifties, most of them in their thirties and forties. Seventy percent were women. Although educators tend to see themselves as poor risk takers, no striking differences emerged between them and the other groups sampled (middle managers and liberal arts graduates).

What did these people regard as major, self-defining risks? Among the 294 participants, nearly 42 percent described risks connected with work; 21 percent talked about interpersonal risks, and 21 percent mentioned a life change that entailed both vocational and interpersonal risks—moving to another city, state, or country. The remainder (16 + percent) listed an interesting medley of other risks. Table 1 shows in somewhat greater detail how these risk perceptions were distributed.

These percentages are cited not to suggest anything about proportions in the general population but simply to give some idea of what a group of rather cautious adults considers personally risky. It is not surprising, of course, that in workshops in which career change was the most salient issue, more than 40 percent of the participants focused on vocational challenges. Nor is it surprising that changing residence should be the single category listed most often, since such a move requires multiple changes—change of physical place, change of support network, change of work or school. As we will see in the data on stress in Chapter 2, such a move tends to cumulate the dangers. We should also note

Table 1   WHAT IS A RISK? ($N = 294$)

TYPE OF RISK	NUMBER DESCRIBING
I. RELOCATING (to change school or job, to be with partner)	61 (20.7%)
II. INTERPERSONAL RISKS	
Divorce or separation (from spouse, mate, or family)	41
Marriage (includes intermarriage, marriage to someone ill, remarriage, or staying in troubled marriage)	8
Confronting family or friends	8
Miscellaneous interpersonal (begin relationship, raise child alone, abort child, have child late)	4
Total Interpersonal	61 (20.7%)
III. PROFESSIONAL/VOCATIONAL RISKS	
Taking more difficult job assignment or special project	48
Reentering school after absence	16
Confronting colleague or boss	12
Quitting job without having another	11
Changing fields	11
Reentering work force after absence	7
Speaking or performing in public	7
Seeking elective office (professional)	5
Miscellaneous professional	6
Total Professional/Vocational	123 (41.8%)
IV. OTHER RISKS	
Traveling alone, remaining abroad for a period	12
Physical risks (rock climbing, scuba diving, etc.)	10
Financial risks (investment, real estate)	9
Miscellaneous other*	18
Total other	49 (16.7%)

*"Miscellaneous other" includes one or two mentions each of the following kinds of items: therapy, helping a suicide victim, cutting a record in Nashville, building a home without training, participating in the death of a parent. Various physical risks that typically were also mentioned by only one or two people included undergoing risky surgery, rock climbing, military combat, scuba diving (for a woman from landlocked Kansas), and piloting her own plane (for a 48-year-old woman who had an intense fear of flying).

that another high-stress situation—divorce—was the most frequently listed item in the category of interpersonal risks that these subjects had chosen to take.

We have already considered some of the perceived characteristics of the risk (extended versus limited, chosen versus imposed). Now we can look at the social and personal variables that influence our perception of dangerous choices, because the question we must always keep in mind is "Risk for whom, and under what conditions?"

What we experience as hazardous depends to some extent on the generally acknowledged and objectively verifiable danger of a given course of action. Even if you are a skilled mountaineer, climbing Mount Everest is perceived as hazardous because it *is* hazardous. So is having a baby for a woman who is diabetic—or doing pushups if you've recently had a heart attack.

While such enterprises are almost universally perceived as dangerous, others may *vary* in their risk value, depending on the context in which they arise: *the social context*—the time and place and reference group in which we move, and *the personal context*—our individual characteristics, such as sex, age, stage of life, temperament, and style. Let's look at each of these contexts.

The Social Context of Risk Perception

Specific life changes are experienced differently at different times and in different generations. When a given behavior is virtually universal or automatic, when its probability of occurrence is close to 100 percent, its subjective riskiness becomes minimized.

Consider the decision to have a child. For centuries this major life event was the result not so much of decision as of accident. Even when birth control methods were highly developed and contraception was therefore within individual control, the choice to have children—usually more than one—was the norm for most couples, at least through the 1960s. Whatever is typical is not seen as highly chancy. Not only is social sanction working toward the choice, but the implicit idea is that if everyone is doing something, it can't be so perilous. In fact, it is usually the *atypical* choice that becomes the dangerous one, for it brings at the very least the risk of social disapproval. Thus, in the 1950s it was risky for a couple to choose *not* to have a child.

But the pendulum has swung widely since then. Contraception has become more efficient, the divorce rate has risen dramatically, abortions have been legalized, and, perhaps more important than all of these, the percentage of women in the work force has doubled. All these trends shaped the women's movement and were in turn impelled by it. Now significant numbers of couples are choosing either not to have children or to defer having them until the time for conception nearly runs out.

This once taken-for-granted decision to become parents now appears more uncertain and more consequential. When it is technically easy not to conceive, when other options than wife/mother are open for women, when fathers are more concerned with parenting—then choosing to have a child becomes a heavily fraught decision. As decisions become more deliberate because society allows more options, uncertainty and anxiety mount. In the terminology of decision theorists, choice becomes more difficult as the number of viable alternatives increases. We have more to consider in making a choice and more to foreclose in settling on a decision.

In previous decades, couples experienced certain anxieties about having children: fear of childbirth itself, apprehension that the child might be defective, anxiety about assuming new responsibility. Given the persistence of the life force, however, these anxieties were small enough for the overwhelming majority of couples to override them.

Today we face a different drama. I have seen more couples than I can count—young men and women in their late twenties to mid-thirties—agonizing over the decision to have a child: Yes or no? If not now, when? If we don't, will we regret it later when we're old and life seems empty? If we do, will we regret it now when we have to give up the freedom we've grown to accept as our due?

And the women ask: How can I juggle two roles (three, counting wife) successfully? How long can I safely wait to make this decision? Will I be too tired and impatient to be a good parent at 38? Or, as one 35-year-old put it, "If you have a pet and find it's too much, you can give it away, but with a baby, that's it. You're stuck for life." The very idea of being "stuck with" a first child was rarely expressed and probably not even consciously entertained (although it must have been unconsciously registered) during the years when having a family was a foregone conclusion.

Demographers tell us that many of the waverers ultimately will have a child—witness the current standing-room-only crowd of older pregnant women in obstetricians' offices. But families may be smaller; more couples will choose to stop at one child. Regardless of the outcome, what I wish to emphasize is the anxiety that now surrounds this formerly almost automatic decision. (The issues are spelled out further in the interview with Jenny and Bob in Chapter 6.)

Time, place, and custom make a significant difference in what is felt to be hazardous. Getting a divorce, for example, is always wrenching, but it would feel much more risky in a Mormon community than in San Mateo, California, where it is the norm for marriages to end in divorce. Similarly, for a homosexual to "come out of the closet" in 1950 would have been experienced as much more anxiety producing than for that step to be taken today, and it would be riskier even now in Sauk Centre than in San Francisco; the individual feels it to be so because the social context exacts much harsher consequences.

The Personal Context of Risk Perception

We have seen that the intensity of a personal risk is largely in the eyes of the beholder. Thus, in addition to the social network that structures our perceptions of what is safe and what is dangerous, forces within the person also determine these feelings. We can distinguish two broad classes of influences: (1) so-called status variables—that is, such characteristics as sex, age, and social class; and (2) personality and temperament.

SEX AND AGE DIFFERENCES

The received wisdom is that women are more conservative and less risk-prone than men and that older people are generally more rigid than younger people. Or, to turn it around, more things appear risky to women and to older people.

Are there any empirical data that bear on these conventional wisdoms? There are, but I must reemphasize that these laboratory studies may have little applicability to actual behavior in real-life situations, where a great deal rides on peoples' choices.

Still, even with their limited generalizability, these studies are at least suggestive. What they suggest is that, when it comes to male/female differences, the stereotype of feminine conservatism is not borne out among adults. In Eleanor Maccoby and Carol Jacklin's comprehensive review of research on sex-role differences, only one study in the entire psychological research literature showed differences in risk-taking between the sexes, and that was between boys and girls aged 11 to 16. (The boys were found to be more likely than the girls to persist in a game of chance with high risk of losses.) No such systematic differences have been observed between adult men and women. The leading researchers on risk taking, Nathan Kogan and Michael Wallach, reported in a summary of their laboratory research that "the overall findings did not by any means offer a neat separation between male risk-takers and female conservatives."

But it is interesting that although Kogan and Wallach and their colleagues found no consistent or striking differences between the sexes, their subjects of both sexes perceived females to be more cautious than males. In other words, whereas a woman would often choose a risky alternative in a laboratory situation, she would predict that other women would respond more cautiously than *she* had; and the men uniformly guessed that women would respond more cautiously than was actually the case. This suggests that the pervasive stereotype about women's cautiousness is not supported by their behavior. It is still likely, however, that men and women regard different areas of life as risky, women finding it easier to take interpersonal risks, men to take vocational risks.

Although overall sex differences in risk taking do not seem to be borne out by research, age differences do receive some empirical support. According to at least one review, older people tend to give more cautious responses in laboratory studies, whether the studies represent betting strategies or choice dilemmas.

Again I must emphasize that these studies have failed to sample adults in midlife or to follow the same individuals across time. They have tended to focus either on the perennial subjects for psychological research—college students—or on people in their late sixties and older. Very little research has sampled people in their thirties, forties, and fifties. These gaps make our knowledge somewhat uncertain.

What we *can* say is that there is some tendency for the elderly to be more cautious. We are more likely to see a given course of action as risky as we grow older, and we are less likely to pursue what is risky. It may be that as people approach old age, their achievement motivation is lower. They may feel that they have less to gain, so why bother risking. But those older people who *do* take risks often feel they have added greatly to their lives.

Age enters into the risks we take in another important way as well—in terms of *which* challenge will arise at a given age or stage of life. Each stage of life has its most usual tasks and challenges, as Erik Erikson and other developmental psychologists have shown us. The risk that adolescents must face, the life change they must initiate, is to disengage from their parents as they find their own identities and establish peer relationships that are deeper and more reciprocal, including those based on sexual attraction as well as friendship. These tasks are filled with hazard and ambivalence. We can see this particularly clearly in the adolescent's cocky forward lurches, followed by painful regressions. These are certainly risky enterprises, but the danger of not working them out, of delaying them to a later life stage, carries even greater risks.

Early adulthood poses different challenges: the risks brought by a search for deep intimacy with a mate, by parenting, and by finding an occupational nest. In late middle age, the life challenge is very different: how to feel productive or, in Erikson's terms, "generative," when we are no longer raising or training the young. It may also include nurturing our own aged parents. In old age, we have the risky obligation to review our lives and find meaning and integrity in them, and eventually to prepare for death.

In sum, these are the major points I want to emphasize:

Although little evidence has been found to support sex differences in risk taking, some suggestive differences emerge when old people are contrasted with young people, the elderly being somewhat less risk-prone.

In addition, the specific kinds of life changes we are likely to face are very much dependent on our stage of life.

Finally, there are many gaps in the available research literature: little work has been done on risk taking in real-life situations, in middle adulthood, or among different social classes.

VARIABLES OF PERSONALITY AND TEMPERAMENT

Again and again in my work as a psychologist, I am struck by the fact that it is not events but our constructions of them that shape our feelings and behavior. In a study of stressful life events, for example, one researcher compared the recent life events of a group of patients who had recently had heart attacks and a nonpatient group of control subjects matched for age and sex. When the two groups were compared, it was found that they did not differ significantly in terms of the objective changes they had experienced. They differed only when the recent events were weighted by the subjects according to *how upsetting* they had been. In other words, reporting events of similar objective magnitude, the two groups had very different perceptions of the stresses imposed by those events.

The *subjective* magnitude of risk depends largely on the individual's preference for stability versus novelty, for security versus freedom. Suppose we represent the amount of change people would ideally choose for themselves as a straight line, with the number of people choosing each point on the line indicated vertically (see Figure 1). The end of the line marked zero would be equivalent to the point of no change at all. This is a purely theoretical point that we never approximate in life. The closest we get to experiencing such uniformity is in our nine-month intrauterine haven, but even in the womb we are rocked by the motions of our inland sea. At the other end of the line is the hypothetical point of constant change. Very few of us feel comfortable at the extremes; most of us fall in the middle range in our preference for change. We seek enough change in our lives to keep things bouncing along and enough permanence to give us solidity. Within our lifetimes we may shift our preferred regions. As we have noted, young people are generally happier in the region of high change; as they get older, they move somewhat toward the region of stability.

Most of us would regard the very low-change/low-risk area as constricted and depressing. And we would regard the opposite region as chaotic and anxiety-producing. How do we navigate between these extremes? How do we find the balance range in which we feel most comfortable—challenged but not stressed? We shall look at these issues more closely in Chapter 3, when we examine styles of risk taking and note that anxious (Style A) risk takers fall toward the left side of the curve, careless (Style C) risk takers fall toward the right side, and balanced (Style B) risk takers prefer the middle region.

What determines our preferred positions on this line of change and risk? They are based on temperament, our constitutions, and our life experiences, including our age. Our constitution and temperament (how quick or slow we are physically, how sensitive or insensitive) are largely determined by our

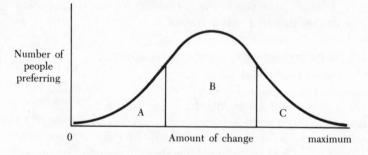

Figure 1

genes. Our life experience teaches us that the world is either a basically friendly place in which it's safe to invite change or a basically hostile one in which change must be avoided. From this matrix of genetic endowment and life experience, we each develop a unique blend of venturesomeness and caution.

As a result of our individual differences in temperament, style, and experience, what is a breeze to one person may be an agony to another, depending on where each person falls in the range of novelty seeking versus permanence seeking or boldness versus caution.

An extremely timid woman who is unsure of her taste and judgment and fearful of "exposure" may find redecorating her living room more distressing than an ebullient, self-assured woman would find moving to a new job in a new city. The fearful redecorator feels she is putting her entire self on the line as she decides what to buy and where to put it. (An interior designer once told me about a client of his who was so insecure that she photographed the way he had placed certain decorative objects on her coffee table so that she would always be sure to put them in the same place.) For someone like this, refurnishing a room is an act of self-definition and self-revelation that gives rise to troublesome questions: What will I unwittingly reveal about myself in this process—that I don't have taste? that I'm stupid? that I can't pull things together decisively? that I'm too cautious and dull? that I have made a terrible mistake? For such a person, virtually every decision becomes an exposure of a badly scarred self that must be concealed. The smallest act becomes pregnant with significance and danger, and a risk that most of us would regard as limited becomes a reverberating danger that persists long after the actual risk is taken (or, probably more often, refused).

Generally, people who are unsure *and* perfectionist are people with low self-esteem who need to get reassurance about themselves by striving for flawless results. They see even the smallest decision as a dangerous test of how worthwhile they are. More confident people will have, in the words of Heinz Hartmann, a larger "conflict-free ego sphere"—an area in which they can feel not that they're "perfect" but simply that they're "good enough" and that being good enough is *itself* good enough.

Our basic cognitive and emotional styles, developed over a lifetime, both reflect and determine how we respond to change. Most of us approach risks in a more or less balanced way. Some people, however, respond extremely, either by massively denying danger or by immobilizing themselves and hence avoiding the problem. Still others adopt strategies of either cautious rumination or thoughtless action.

These styles, because they are so deep-seated, are very hard to change. We cannot readily change our basic anxiety level, our tendency to be impulsive or reflective, our basic conservatism versus openness to change. But we can learn to become aware of our own style and make certain allowances, to watch out for self-defeating patterns and correct for them in subtle ways that make important differences.

Furthermore, in order to take a risk, we may have to *reframe* a situation to give it a different meaning. A woman who has to confront being divorced, for example, may learn to rely briefly on a narrowing of focus, a temporary tunnel vision that enables her to get through one day at a time until she feels solid enough to use a wide-angle lens again. Similarly, the teacher we discussed earlier in this chapter changed the character of her risk in teaching a demonstration class by reframing it as her choice, rather than as a total imposition. This kind of redefining, according to sociologist Leonard Pearlin, "does not eradicate the problem itself; it controls and shapes the meaning that the problem has for the individual so that its stressful effects are buffered."

I now wish to do some reframing myself. So far, I have filled in the outlines of personal risk: its essential characteristics, the undertakings people perceive to be risky, and what influences these perceptions. In Chapter 2, I will put personal risk in the larger frame in which it belongs—the frame of change. Every time we take a risk, we are confronting both internal and external change—changing our circumstances, changing ourselves. To understand why risk is hard, we need to see why change is hard. To learn why risking is gratifying, we need to see how change brings growth.

Chapter 2
The Risk of Change:
Losses and Gains

All our lives long, every day and every hour we are
engaged in the process of accommodating our changed and
unchanged selves to changed and unchanged surroundings;
living, in fact, is nothing else than this process of accommodation; when we fail in it a little we are stupid, when
we fail flagrantly we are mad, when we suspend it temporarily we sleep, when we give up the attempt altogether
we die.

Samuel Butler, *The Way of All Flesh*

Every personal risk we take in life—from our first step away from mother
through our first day at school, our first intimate relationship, a marriage, a
divorce, the birth of a child, launching a career, moving to a new city, planning
for retirement, preparing for death—every personal risk represents a change.
Every time we venture on a new life course, we face losses and gains. In taking
the kinds of personal risks I will consider, we are in effect inviting change. To
invite change takes courage and hope; to see it through takes skill.

In order to understand risk, then, we need to ask the following questions:
Why is change difficult? Why is it essential? What are the costs? What are the
payoffs? And finally, given the difficulties, how can we make change easier for
ourselves? This chapter will sketch some preliminary answers to these
questions, which I will take up more fully and concretely in the rest of the
book.

CHANGE AS THE LAW OF LIFE

The preeminent philosopher of change, Heraclitus, wrote centuries ago, "You
cannot step into the same river twice, for other waters are ever flowing on."
Perhaps you can't even step into the same river *once*, for even as you immerse
your foot, the river is changing and you are changing.

From galaxies to organelles, all is in flux. Biologists tell us that the cells of our body go through a complete cycle of change every seven years. If we could compress the eons on our planet, if we could stand out in space and look at our own galaxy through time-lapse photography, what would we see? We'd see constellations born out of gases and constellations disintegrating. Our own tiny planet—that spectacular blue marble that was revealed to us during the moon landings—would display its course of bulging, erupting, condensing—glaciers forming and melting, the earth's rind furrowing and bunching, land masses breaking off from each other.

The evolution of living things on our planet has a similar thrust, as described by Allen Wheelis, a psychiatrist and contemporary philosopher of change:

> Particles become animate.... Minute creatures writhe in warm oceans...virus becomes bacteria, becomes algae, becomes fern.... Amoeba reaches out soft blunt arms in ceaseless motion to find the world.... Anemone becomes squid, becomes fish; wiggling becomes swimming, becomes crawling; fish becomes slug, becomes lizard; crawling becomes walking, becomes running, becomes flying.

In living organisms, the absence of change is death. We can see this on the largest scale—the evolutionary failure of the dinosaurs to adapt to changing climatic conditions—and on the smallest. Consider, for example, the visual apparatus of humans. Even when we try very hard to fixate on an object steadily, we produce tiny, totally involuntary eye movements; their function is to expose constantly shifting groups of retinal receptors to the light stimulus. Experiments in which the effects of this movement have been negated—so-called stopped-image procedures—yield an amazing result: the image disappears. Paradoxically, seeing things steadily requires constant eye movement.

THE ACCELERATING PACE OF CHANGE

Change may be the order of life, but never has it been visited on us so massively and relentlessly as in our century. Wherever we look, we find confirmation of this central fact of life. Economist Kenneth Boulding put it graphically in describing 1900, the year of his birth, as "a median strip running down the highway of history." The world of today, he wrote, is as different from that of 1900 as that world was from the time of the Caesars. This is true for most indices we might choose to use, and particularly for the palpable, visible things we see around us, the fruits of science and technology.

Another way to illustrate this notion is demonstrated by Alvin Toffler in *Future Shock*—a primer of "futurology," the new branch of human study aimed at predicting both the nature and the extent of change. Toffler divided the last 50,000 years of human history into "lifetimes" of 62 + years, as a way to make eons understandable on some human scale. He noted that, of the 800 lifetimes produced by this division (62 into 50,000), a staggering proportion—

650—were spent in caves. Toffler points out:

> Only during the last seventy lifetimes has it been possible to communicate
> effectively from one lifetime to another, as writing made it possible to do. Only
> during the last six lifetimes did masses of men ever see a printed word. Only during
> the last four has it been possible to measure time with any precision. Only in the
> last two has anyone anywhere used an electric motor. And the overwhelming
> majority of all the material goods we use in daily life today have been developed
> within the present, the 800th, lifetime.

These changes in communication and technology have made possible the so-
called knowledge explosion. One index of this explosion, Toffler tells us, is the
amount of time taken to produce a given number of books. In 1500 it took about
a year to produce a thousand different books; by 1950, a thousand new titles
were being produced every three and a half days; and by the 1970s, the world's
presses were spewing out more than a thousand new titles *every day*. Advances
in information technology now enable us to put the contents of whole libraries
on tiny silicon chips. And the knowledge industry—the gathering, storing,
retrieving, and disseminating of information—now employs nearly 50 percent
of the U.S. work force.

This statistic illustrates that the nature of the work in which most people
are engaged—at least in the developed nations of the globe—has shifted
dramatically. For the first time in the United States, in western Europe, and in
Japan—that harbinger of the twenty-first century—agriculture is no longer the
dominant mode of employment that it was throughout the nineteenth century.
Today only 3.5 percent of the U.S. population works as farmers. For the first
time, the burden of manual labor has been lifted. We now have more people in
the service occupations—administration, education, research, communica-
tions, retail trade, and personal services (72 percent)—than in manual labor
and agriculture (28 percent). Thus, whereas, in 1890, 4 percent of the U.S.
population worked in information collection and dissemination and 46 percent
worked in agriculture, the proportions have now been almost exactly reversed.

This trend will continue as the knowledge industry expands and as we
witness the further growth of a "new class" or "new elite"—the affluent and
educated group of specialists, presently estimated at between five and ten
million people, with advanced degrees and specialized professional or technical
skills that are honed to the increasingly stringent demands of technology and
change.

THE OTHER SIDE OF PROGRESS

You may say that this trend looks like progress—and it is. We know more and
more about our world and our universe; we can study the braided ringlets of
Saturn, we can move mountains and make rain, we can reduce poverty and
hunger, and we can liberate men and women from the yoke of crushing labor.

We can do all these things, but we pay a price. Ultimately, there are "no gains without pains." The pain of this change and, more important, of its constant acceleration hits all of us, both collectively and as individuals. We see it particularly clearly in the family. The extended family—grandparents, parents, children, and close relatives all living near each other and supporting each other—is as hard to find as a Model T. Even the prototypical nuclear family of a few decades ago—father, nonworking mother, and children all under the same roof—is a fast-dying species. We are seeing more and more single-parent families (the proportion has doubled since 1960, with 12 percent of white children and 40 percent of black children now living in single-parent households). Nearly one in two marriages ends in divorce, and "blends" or "reconstituted families" (with children who are "his," "hers," and "theirs") are giving family sociologists much to study and family members much to negotiate.

We see such signs of transience everywhere: The average length of residence in one place is now five years. The average American now can expect to change jobs five to seven times in the course of his or her working life—and these are more and more often totally different career paths, not mere changes of place of employment. Changes in technology and in values produce changes in living arrangements, which then set up their own currents that buffet the individual. Change seems to beget change at an ever-accelerating pace.

I am not writing this as an indictment of change or as a jeremiad (as has become fashionable) against the rootless society we seem to be producing. I *am* suggesting that every benefit carries a price tag. Thus, the climate in which every kind of life-style is permissible can be regarded, on the one hand, as a testament to openness and pluralism and, on the other hand, as a symptom of chaos. Is this the worst of times? Sometimes it seems so. But if we turn the kaleidoscope a few degrees, without changing any of the pieces, we may get a design that suggests that this is also the best of times. Any simple evaluation falsifies the picture. We live in difficult, interesting, demanding times—times that require constant changes in our adaptation. We pay for the increase in options with increased anxiety about our roles and about how we can hold our ground while the earth we stand on is trembling.

We can feel the tremors in the social disorganization we see all around us. Although experts had predicted a drop in the national crime rate during 1979 and into the 1980s based on sheer demography—a drop in the number of young people in the 15- to 24-year-old age group that traditionally has committed the most crimes—in fact the rate of serious crimes rose by 9 percent during the first half of 1979. A writer commenting on this statistic in *The New York Times* of October 28, 1979, suggests that "the surge of violence and defiance of the law that began in the 1960s has become an indelible part of the social fabric and...the causes are much more complex than was once believed." The years of the Great Depression and World War II seem to have fostered a sense of community that lasted into the 1960s and brought relatively low crime rates. The 1960s and 1970s were unusually turbulent, and in 1978 the murder rate was three times higher than it was in 1938.

We could draw an equally grim picture of the incidence of mental illness and breakdown. Even more telling, perhaps, is the increase in stress-related, serious, chronic diseases: hypertension, peptic ulcer, colitis. In *Social Stress and Chronic Illness*, Dodge and Martin note that "the diseases of our times, namely the chronic diseases, are etiologically linked with excessive stress, and in turn this stress is a product of specific socially structured situations inherent in the organization of modern technological societies." Moreover, the view now gaining acceptance is that stress is a predisposing factor not only in diseases that are clearly psychosomatic or chronic but also possibly in injuries and acute infections.

THE PAIN OF CHANGE: LIFE CHANGE AND STRESS

We hear more and more about stress research today—in professional symposia and articles, in the popular press, and on TV talk shows. No book on any related subject (and related subjects may range as far afield as walking for health) is complete without its table of numerical weights of stressful life events. The American Psychiatric Association has officially recognized the importance of stress by including "severity of psychosocial stressors" as a supplementary dimension to be used in describing the psychiatric status of individuals.

Research on stress originated in the 1930s with the work of Walter B. Cannon, a physiologist, and more especially that of Hans Selye, a physician-researcher who labeled the response to stress as the "general adaptation syndrome"—a group of bodily reactions to harmful aspects of the environment.

Building on this pioneer work, over the last 15 years an increasing number of scientists have begun studying the relationship between life changes and illness.* These life changes—such as bereavement, marriage, divorce, loss of a job—require that the individual alter his or her ongoing life pattern. The individual responds to these changes with physiological and psychological reactions that eventually may take the form of clinical symptoms of a disease.

The beginning work in this area of *life-events research* was done by Thomas Holmes, a psychiatrist, and Richard Rahe, a psychologist, who sought to demonstrate that the onset of illness is associated with a recent increase in the number of life changes that require that the individual respond in new ways and, moreover, that these changes are cumulative—that is, the more such events a person experiences in a given period, the greater the likelihood of illness shortly thereafter.

Briefly, Holmes and Rahe first constructed the Social Readjustment Rating

*Overviews and critiques of these studies can be found in Judith Rabkin and Elmer L. Struening, "Life Events, Stress, and Illness," *Science* 194 (3 December 1976); and in Barbara Dohrenwend and Bruce Dohrenwend (eds.), *Stressful Life Events* (New York: Wiley, 1974).

Scale, which consisted of a long list of life events, ranging from "death of a family member" to "taking a vacation." This scale was submitted to large samples of raters in the United States, Japan, and Western Europe for rating as to relative severity of the stress they would produce. The American group included Hispanics and blacks. It is interesting that, even when groups as diverse as Americans and Japanese were compared, agreement about the rank order of severity of these life changes was fairly high. In a commonly used version of the scale, the highest rating—100 life-change units—is given to the death of a close family member (a spouse or a child) and the lowest score—11 units—to a minor traffic violation. Marriage falls at the midpoint—50; divorce at 73; being fired from a job at 47. An unwanted pregnancy for a woman turns out to be about equal in stress to being drafted for a man. (Pregnancy itself is one of those events that illustrate the importance of context: for an infertile couple who have wanted a child for years it has a much different meaning than it has for an unmarried adolescent girl or for a family with six children and an unemployed father.)

This rating scale was then used to construct the Schedule of Recent Experience, in which the respondent is asked to check off life events that have occurred during a specified time period (e.g., the last six months, one year, or two years). Scores are assigned, based on the rating scale, and these scores are then summed—on the assumption that the effect of stress is cumulative. The initial work showed that patients who currently were suffering from tuberculosis, heart disease, skin disease, or hernia had had a significantly higher number of life changes during the preceding two years than a matched control group had.

To get around the criticism that people who are currently ill may perceive that more bad things had happened to them in the past, Holmes and Rahe and their co-workers carried out a series of predictive studies in which their subjects first were asked to check off stressful events for the preceding time period and then were followed medically for a succeeding period. Subjects for this research included 50 medical students followed for two years, 2500 naval officers and enlisted men on three Navy cruisers followed for six months, and 100 football players observed during a football season. In every case, the subjects who reported the greatest changes during the preceding period had the highest incidence and greatest severity of illness (in the case of football players, injuries) in the following period. The Navy cruiser study was particularly interesting because of the large number of subjects and because sick-bay records were relatively complete. During the first month at sea, the subjects in the high-change group reported 90 percent more first illnesses than the low-change group; they continued to report more illness during each month of the six-month cruise; moreover, their illnesses were more serious than those in the low-change group.

How can we put these findings in a context that will be useful for our discussion of risk taking? We can begin by asking what makes a change a stressor. In answering this question, three categories must be considered: (1) the nature and amount of change; (2) the resources of the individual; and (3) the social support system of the person experiencing the change. Let's look briefly at each of these categories.

The Nature of the Change

There is some debate about which is more important in producing stress: how massive the change is or how undesirable it is. Some people hold that large-scale change is disruptive no matter how much it is desired. According to this view, a promotion to a new job is stressful even when it represents a desired outcome. Others feel that the undesirability of a change may be more disruptive than its size. But even desired changes, when large enough (e.g., a major promotion), will produce stress. Most of the risks we will look at, although they are self-initiated and therefore presumably desirable, nevertheless can lead to physical and psychological unease.

Another dimension related to the stressfulness of a change is how much it is perceived to be under the individual's own control. I have talked about this in considering the chosen versus the imposed risk. To give this issue more reality, we can look at the recently revised *Diagnostic Manual of the American Psychiatric Association* (known to professionals as DSM-III). This manual now holds that assessing the stress level under which an individual operates is an important part of defining his or her psychological function, and it recommends rating the severity of the stress in terms of "the amount of change in the individual's life caused by the stress, the degree to which the event is desired and under the individual's control, and the number of stressors." Generally, rating of stress is made based on experiences of the previous year. Table 2 gives examples of the stress levels. It is obvious that these examples cannot be applied across the board, since, as we have already noted, events such as a

Table 2   STRESS LEVELS

CODE	STRESS LEVEL TERM	ADULT EXAMPLE
1	None	No apparent psychosocial stressor
2	Minimal	Minor violation of the law; small bank loan
3	Mild	Argument with neighbor; change in work hours
4	Moderate	New career; death of close friend; pregnancy
5	Severe	Serious illness in self or family; major financial loss; marital separation; birth of child
6	Extreme	Death of close relative; divorce
7	Catastrophic	Concentration camp experience; devastating natural disaster

Reprinted with permission from American Psychiatric Association, *Quick Reference to the Diagnostic Criteria from DSM-III* (Washington, D.C.: American Psychiatric Association, 1980), pp. 14–15.

pregnancy or the birth of a child can have totally different stress values, depending on their context. The *Diagnostic Manual* takes into account the number of stressors by suggesting that the severity rating "should reflect the summed effect of all the psychosocial stressors that are listed."

The Resources of the Individual

As we have seen, it is not the events themselves but the individual's perception of them as harmful or threatening that makes the difference between a neutral or positive event and a stressor. This is because we are not merely passive receivers of change but active responders, seeking to reduce stress by coping as best we can. Our capacity to do this depends on the kinds of personal characteristics we talked about in Chapter 1—sensitivity levels, intelligence, temperament, defensive structures, flexibility. It also depends on our sense of relationship to our fates—the sense either that our behavior is largely within ourselves or that it is primarily imposed by circumstance. People who are better endowed in all these respects do better with large changes.*

Furthermore, practice or familiarity with a particular stressful event leads to easier adaptation in similar instances. It may also be, as my research on risk taking suggests, that the more we experience ourselves as dealing successfully with *any* major stress, the greater the likelihood that we can handle some *other*, unrelated stress well. In other words, there may be a generalized as well as a specific effect of practice in dealing with major changes.

I want to reemphasize the importance of the context in determining whether or not an event is stressful, just as in determining whether or not a choice is risky. We have already noted how the birth of a child can be more or less stressful depending on the context. Similarly, retirement holds different meanings depending on the person's previous investment in work and relationship to leisure. For some people, who have always had interests apart from work, retirement provides an eagerly anticipated opportunity to develop previously underused parts of the self; for others, who have been almost exclusively defined by their work, retirement may open a dread void of purposelessness and despair.

Social Supports

We must also consider the importance of social status and social networks in modifying stress. People may lack support networks for external reasons (for example, when they have moved away from home and family to a new city) or

---

*A relevant recent study by Suzanne Kobasa and her colleagues first rated a large group of middle- and upper-level male executives for their "hardiness"—their commitment to themselves, sense of control over their world, and tendency to regard change as stimulating rather than threatening. Stressful life events were recorded for these men over the next five-year period. It was found that men who had scored high on hardiness suffered significantly less physical illness under high stress than did men who had fewer of the so-called resistance resources.

for internal ones (because anxiety causes them to withdraw from human contacts). Studies have shown that social isolates—people who live alone and have few or no friends and no institutional or organizational ties—are more susceptible to disease, as are people from low-status minorities. Stress is also more common among minority members who exist in particularly small numbers in their communities; thus, a Chinese family in a town in the Texas Panhandle, unlike a Chinese family in San Francisco, has a skimpy network of support and affiliation. Finally, disparities of status within an individual are often likely to lead to anxiety and ill health, as, for example, when a woman with a Ph.D. in history is working as a bank teller or when a man is advanced to a position that requires more than he feels his training has prepared him for.

In conclusion, the research on stress indicates that some life events will be traumatic for almost everyone—the catastrophic events, such as natural disasters, and the irreversible events, such as the death of a close family member. But in the less severe categories, the individual response is more complicated than can be suggested by an average on a scale. How a given person will respond to a major change will depend, as we have seen, on a subtle interaction among (1) the nature and magnitude of the change, (2) the individual's resiliency, and (3) the individual's support system. These factors are important because they apply as much to chosen risks as to the imposed ones that bulk so large in stress research.

In summary, the following major conclusions from the research on life events are most significant for our growing understanding of personal risk taking:

The effects of change are cumulative. Thus, for example, moving to a new city—which entails changing one's living quarters, one's job, and one's friends—will generally impose more stress than staying in the same place and merely changing one's job.

Positive changes can also be stressful. We know that vacations and promotions can bring stress. Someone who has initiated a combination of changes—such as starting a new love affair, getting promoted, and buying a larger house—may undergo significant anxiety, even though all these changes were highly desired. We will better understand why this might occur when we talk about change as loss.

Individuals differ dramatically in how much stress they experience and in how well they process stress-provoking change. Although the most severe life changes are almost universally felt to be stressful, individual differences in capacity to cope are highly important when it comes to experiencing lesser changes as stress-producing.

Practice plays a part in our ability to confront and manage change. The more experience we have had in dealing successfully with change, the readier we are to master future change.

Our network of family, friends, and colleagues (that is, our social support system) *can significantly modify our perception and handling of major life change*. This is important because, as we shall see, one of the crucial steps in risk taking is the active enlistment of support from the people who matter to us.

Why Risk Is Stressful: Change as Loss

So far, I have spoken mostly of correlations and associations: X amount of life change is associated with Y amount of illness or maladaptation. To look a little deeper, however, we must ask *why:* Why is change hard? Why is change perceived as risky, especially since it is so ubiquitous and so much built into our lives at every level, from ganglions to galaxies? Why, indeed, are people resistant to change—for aren't we all change resistors as well as change inviters, risk avoiders as well as risk seekers?

A humanistic psychologist recently told me, somewhat ruefully, that she thought the human potential movement might have oversold the possibility of quick, dramatic change. Everyone is in favor of self-actualization and self-transformation, but most of us who work intensively with people as patients or clients know that *major* changes in the self are rare and that most internal change happens gradually.

Resistance in therapy, as in real life, represents a conservative tendency that warns us about the costs of change. What are the costs? What are we afraid of? What do we stand to lose?

At its simplest, any change brings a loss of the known. A case in point is Louise, a woman seen in therapy by a colleague of mine. Louise was one of those fat women with "such a pretty face." She was grossly obese at the outset of treatment, but a year later she had lost more than a hundred pounds and was extremely attractive, if only barely recognizable. She complained, however, that she was unprepared for the response of her friends, many of whom greeted her not with approval but with outrage. "What's happened? What have you done to yourself?" a number of them asked, as though she had attacked them personally. She was unsettled by this response, but she later came to see that *she* had unsettled *them;* her marked physical change had threatened their basic sense of *their* continuity.

We go to great lengths to maintain our sense of continuous selfhood, even when it means repeating patterns that are self-defeating but as familiar as our skin. We have had ample testimony of the panic that can occur in extreme forms of loss of continuity, as in drug-induced alterations of consciousness or in psychosis (whose most eloquent chronicler is R. D. Laing in *The Divided Self*). Although some people may experiment happily with altered states of consciousness, most of us find such states deeply disturbing if they are protracted, particularly if they appear to be beyond our control.

One of the most upsetting alterations in our sense of self-continuity comes from physical illness and hospitalization. Most of us go along feeling pretty much at home in our bodies, pretty much able to incorporate them into our sense of self. Being physically ill and hospitalized changes all that. The body becomes peremptory; it takes over. We become not an embodied self but a physical object—a thing to be poked, peered at, prodded, injected, catheterized. No wonder our noncorporeal part is screaming in outrage, "I'm here, too." This reversal of the usual balance is deeply unsettling to our continuous identity. As W. H. Auden put it in his poem "Surgical Ward":

For who, when healthy, can become a foot?*

Any large and sudden change threatens us not only with the loss of continuity of ourselves but also with the loss of the known world we carry with us. Beth, a talented young jeweler who has been in therapy for several years, put it this way:

Being stuck, being depressed is awful. But it's safe. It's—well—it's like walking around in the dark in a room you hate. Say it's a room in your parents' house that you've known since you were a kid. You can tell in the dark where every table, every nicked chair is, every picture, every ashtray. You could walk it blindfolded without bumping or scraping. It may be an ugly room, a drab room, but it's *familiar*.

But when you change—when you take a risk or do something that's way out of character for you—it's different. It's like being thrust in the dark into a furnished room that is unfamiliar. This is probably a more interesting room, one you may get to like because it's going to be all yours. But the furniture is strange. You don't know where anything is yet. You might bump into something knobby and hard, you might trip and fall.

Change—and taking a risk means *inviting change*—blurs the familiar outlines of our world and requires that we move on, literally or figuratively, leaving people and places behind, including parts of ourselves.

What we leave behind is a certain construction of reality that has given meaning to our lives. In his profound book, *Loss and Change*, Peter Marris, a British social scientist, discusses the deep conservative impulse that runs through all of us. He says that although human beings are the most adaptable and ingenious of all living creatures, they also need to defend insistently the continuity that enables them to see their lives as meaningful, as coherent and predictable. Predictability of our own behavior and that of others requires that we put new experiences into an established context of "habits, principles, purposes, and attachments." Marris adds: "We assimilate new experiences by placing them in the context of a familiar, reliable construction of reality. This structure in turn rests not only on the regularity of events themselves, but on the continuity of their *meaning*" [italics mine]. When we lose the continuity of meaning, we lose the continuity of self.

Choosing examples from research on topics as diverse as the bereavement of young widows and urban renewal in Boston, London, and Lagos, Nigeria,

*From "Sonnets from China, XIV," in *Collected Poems*, by W. H. Auden, edited by Edward Mendelson (New York: Random House, 1976), p. 154. Copyright 1976 by Random House, Inc.

Marris shows that every disruptive life change—*even one that is presumably desirable* (such as slum clearance, which offers new, clean living quarters)—imposes similar demands:

> The need to re-establish continuity, to work out an interpretation of oneself and the world which preserves, despite estrangement, the thread of meaning; the ambivalence of this task, as it swings between conflicting impulses; the need to articulate the stages of its resolution; and the risk of lasting disintegration if the process is not worked out."

Marris takes bereavement as a model for illustrating the reaction to all profound change, personal and social. He asserts that "the fundamental crisis of bereavement arises not from the loss of others but from the loss of self—the loss of purpose, of interest, and above all, of meaning. How we recapture that meaning is all-important. Mourning rituals enable the bereaved to recapture meaning by withdrawing and giving the dead person a central place in their lives, to recover the past while acknowledging the irrevocability of the loss. Then a reintegrative process takes place slowly and painfully. Mourning requires us to transcend two tempting but destructive impulses: to deny the loss by looking only ahead or to mummify the past and refuse to surrender it and move on.

The U-shaped course of completed mourning can be described as withdrawal, grieving, reintegration, and return. Thus, following early widowhood, Marris tells us, the widow progresses from actually envisioning and talking to her dead husband to

> thinking about what he would have said and done and from there to planning her own and her children's future in terms of what he would have wished, until finally the wishes become her own, and she no longer consciously refers them to him. Thus grief is mastered, not by ceasing to care for the dead, but by abstracting what was fundamentally important in the relationship and rehabilitating it.

What can we learn from these reflections? First, every profound change—even a desired change—implies a loss. That loss is experienced, above all, as a loss of meaning and a loss of continuity of self. We can recover from such loss by creating bridges that link us to what we have been and what has had meaning for us. Finally, to cope with the loss brought by change, we must steer between two opposing temptations: the desire to cling perpetually to what is past and the desire to bury it. We must chart a course between melancholia (as Freud so brilliantly distinguished it from true mourning) and denial, learning both how to preserve and how to let go of our past.

In dealing with risk taking, which is the seeking out of potentially dangerous situations, our fear is not only that we will lose or abandon the known (especially our known world of meaning) but that we will fail to gain what we seek from the unknown. Thus every change, even the most wanted, carries with it the faint autumnal odor of loss, like burning leaves. Those who cannot face such loss try to stay put or to deny that they have changed. *But there is a loss implied in staying put as well,* because for living organisms, staying put is really moving backward. When we cease to grow, we shrivel. We can either constrict our experience or we can extend it and try to make it part of us. The first alternative often leads to *depression,* the second to *anxiety.* We repeatedly choose between these alternatives. As I shall emphasize again and again in this book, however, mastering the anxiety of venturing promotes new levels of growth.

THE LIMITS OF CHANGE

Just as our conservative impulse is deep and enduring, so we all experience some kind of counterthrust—the need to expand, to extend ourselves, to master new challenges. In the rest of this book, it is this positive thrust that will concern us—this thrust that makes people seek out the unknown, take on difficult tasks, test themselves, and push themselves. Before getting to the specifics, we need to understand risk taking in a more general way by asking how much change is too much and how much is enough. What kind of process is necessary to assimilate the new into the old? I will try to illuminate these questions by using illustrations from the equilibrating mechanisms of the human body and from organisms that are subjected to too great and too little change. These suggestive examples will provide us with ballast in our thinking about risk taking.

The Human Body as a Processor of Change

Walter B. Cannon, the physiologist whose work spurred the research on stress and life change, wrote in his book, *The Wisdom of the Body* (a title that is both a warning and a celebration):

> Our bodies are made up of extraordinarily unstable material, Pulses of energy so minute that very delicate methods are required to measure them course along our nerves. On reaching muscles they find there a substance so delicately sensitive to slight disturbance that...it may discharge in a powerful movement. Our sense organs are responsive to almost incredibly minute stimulations. Only recently have men been able to make apparatus which could even approach the sensitiveness of our organs of hearing. The sensory surface in the nose is affected by vanillin one part by weight in 10,000,000 parts of air.

This extreme instability of bodily response, this acute sensitivity to change, makes us wonder how such a system could persist throughout eons. One would think it would resemble artist Paul Klee's vision of a tremulous "twittering machine." It is not, of course, and that is because, over the same eons, the body has developed an equally exquisite system of equilibrium, of setting its own thermostat.

Cannon gave a number of examples of such corrective mechanisms in our bodies. During heavy exercise, we generate so much heat that muscle tissues would quickly take on the consistency of hard-boiled egg were it not for the heat dissipation system the body has evolved (mainly through sweating). Similarly, when our blood pressure falls and the oxygen supply is threatened, a nerve in the carotid artery sends messages to the vasomotor center, and the blood supply is automatically raised.

Ths idea of the body as an equilibrium-preserving mechanism was first described by the nineteenth-century French physiologist, Claude Bernard, who spoke of our *milieu intérieur,* our constant internal environment. To preserve this internal climate, we not only must maintain a relatively stable temperature in our cells but must also keep stable the chemical composition of fluids that surround them. One aspect of this process is described by Jonathan Miller in *The Body in Question:*

> Multi-cellular animals. . . can enclose and defend an inland sea whose chemical composition is supervised and regulated by the kidney. When surplus water lowers the concentration of body fluid, the kidney automatically lets out an extra volume of dilute urine; when water is in short supply, the urine becomes scanty and concentrated. The system exercises differential control of the retention and release of mineral salts as well: it can hold back sodium and eliminate surplus potassium. By orchestrating these and many other reactions, the kidney creates a favourable constancy for the living cells of the body.

This principle of servomechanisms—self-regulating devices through which some of the energy of a functioning system is used to offset too-great fluctuations in its own behavior—was first described in mechanical systems such as the steam engine. But the work of physiologists like Bernard and Cannon showed that it applies as much to our living bodies as to any other system whose efficiency demands a steady state.

Our body's network of self-regulating mechanisms is truly awe-inspiring. Our external milieu may vary from 30 degrees below zero Fahrenheit to 120 degrees Fahrenheit, yet our brain cells, as Miller put it, "are enclosed in a self-regulated tropics."

However—and this is the point I am leading to—*there are limits to the adaptability of the body.* Although we are built to withstand external temperatures as high as 261 degrees Fahrenheit for very short intervals without an increase in body temperature, if we run a fever of 106 degrees for any extended period, severe and permanent destruction of our brain cells will result. The wisdom of the body is that, although we are remarkably subtle and flexible organisms, *there are limits to how much change we can assimilate.* This is a major lesson for us as risk takers.

Too Much Change: The Case of the Traumatized Puppies

We have already looked at some of the reasearch that dealt with response to large life changes. Ethical considerations prevent researchers from introducing truly massive changes in controlled ways into the lives of human organisms.

Since the strictures on animal research are not so binding, however, there has been some research on what happens to nonhuman infants when they are subjected to sudden large change. In one such study, conducted by John Fuller, beagle and terrier puppies were kept in individual cages, 60 centimeters square, for the first 21 days of their lives. The puppies were fed and watered and had their waste removed without receiving either visual or tactile stimulation. Then, after 21 days, they were let out into a walled-in arena that was 3.5 meters square (to the puppies, a terrifyingly large space, 34 times the size of their home cage). In this arena, the puppies' orientation and movement responses were measured, as well as their responses to the person who was handling them for the first time, to toys introduced into the arena, and to another puppy brought into the space. How did the previously isolated puppies behave when confronted by this overwhelming change? They froze, struggled, howled, and defecated. In short, they were disoriented and traumatized.

Although such studies reflect the importance of so-called critical periods during which infant organisms must receive certain kinds of stimulation for specific functions to develop, they also suggest that too much change coming all at once can be devastating. In normal development, as Fuller points out, "the environment opens up gradually to a growing puppy as its motor and sensory capacities carry it out of the nest into the world." So it was not surprising that in control studies, whatever was introduced to decrease the amount of change from the original barren, confined world of the cage to the complex, vast world of the arena reduced the degree of trauma to the puppy. Putting a window in the original isolation cage, for example, enabling the puppy to see the enriched world it would later enter, reduced the shock. Similarly, attempts to comfort and reassure the animals—by stroking and handling them—made the transition less stressful. We could translate this into human risk-related terms by saying that the puppies' anxiety was reduced through *information* and through *support*.

This animal research has relevance to risk taking in suggesting the following:

> We cannot take change in massive doses; we become traumatized when the change is too great or comes too quickly.
>
> Anything we can do to anticipate, foreshadow, or rehearse a part of the change makes the new situation less disruptive.
>
> Reduction of anxiety in major change requires both information and emotional support.

Too Little Change

What is too much change depends, as we have seen, not only on individual differences in flexibility but also on what we have been used to. Fuller's puppies experienced the change as disruptive because it was too sudden and too massive. Or, looked at another way, it was too much because their previous world had been too confined and too changeless. Studies of adult subjects who are exposed to periods of stimulus deprivation (being placed in tepid water in isolation tanks, with no visual or auditory input) show that lack of stimulation has its own devastating consequences; these subjects experience marked anxiety after a period of time and may begin hallucinating.

Studies of institutionalized children, beginning with the work of René Spitz, have indicated that, in addition to needing constant and dependable caretaking, infants need a stimulating environment for growth and development. Indeed, such stimulation is as necessary for growth as is meeting their bodily needs for food and drink. Infants living in settings of environmental barrenness develop symptoms ranging from apathy and retardation to a failure to thrive, or "wasting syndrome," that may lead to death.

What happens at the limits is clear. What is not so clear—what each of us must determine for ourselves—is how far along the line of change we feel most alive and where we feel most comfortable. Unfortunately, these are often two different points. The comfort zone is safe; the zone of aliveness is risky. We need to modulate the two to find a balance range. One way to approach this modulation is to understand change as taking place within secure structure.

A MODEL FOR GROWTH: CHANGE WITHIN STRUCTURE

We have seen the disruptive consequences of change that is too massive and sudden, on the one hand, and of the absence of novelty and stimulation, on the other. What we require is a balance. Just as we need to conserve and consolidate, we experience a counterthrust—the need to expand, to extend ourselves, to master new challenges. These polar strivings can be reconciled by positing an *optimal amount of change—the amount that can be dealt with by existing structures*. We will first look at this process through the earliest attempts of infants to explore from a secure base.

Attachment and Exploratory Behavior in Infants

In healthy infants with a good enough ordinary environment, physical maturation takes place according to a biological timetable, with change occurring as the already developed structures allow. Thus, walking does not precede crawling, and crawling doesn't occur before sitting; instead, each activity appears to build on its predecessors. The same pattern applies, as psychologist Jean Piaget has showed us, to cognitive development. Piaget's work has demonstrated that the level of mental structure children have available determines what they can respond to in their environment. A five-year-old girl, for instance, has the mental structure (Piaget's term is *schema*) to recognize that changing the shape of a ball of clay does not change the amount—a recognition that is unavailable to her three-year-old brother; but she does not yet have the cognitive structures that will permit her to think in abstract terms about ideas or propositions.

As John Flavell put it in his masterly summary of Piaget's work, "the child cannot accommodate to novelties which ongoing structures cannot assimilate, and yet structural change cannot proceed without the proper measure of stimulation from the milieu—no change until the child is in some sense ready, but also no change unless, when ready, something comes his way." The balance and interplay of structure and stimulation—of stability and novelty—seem to be all-important. The principle of change within structure applies to social and emotional as well as physiological and cognitive development.

Developmental research has shown that growth takes place only when the physical or psychological structure supporting it is secure. That is what happens when the infant, at one year or a little later, begins taking his first stumbling steps: he launches himself forth somewhat hesitantly, with frequent glances back to his mother or even a return to home base. Like the Greek god Janus, he looks both forward and back. And it is the knowledge that his mother (or other care giver) is dependably present that enables him to venture.

Substantial research related to this pattern of attachment and exploration (which we might think of as the veering between safety and danger, between caution and daring) has been done by Mary Ainsworth and her associates. They studied the behavior of one-year-olds whom they put in a congenial but novel situation—a playroom with toys—first with the mother present, then with a stranger present, then alone. They observed several patterns of responding among these one-year-olds. One of these—the attached pattern—seemed most clearly adaptive. It was observed in children who explored differently depending on the situation (i.e., greater exploration when in the safety of mother's presence) and who seemed to have strong, unambivalent ties to their mothers. They maintained frequent eye contact or physical contact with the mother but were able to move out on their own; they were affected by her absence and greeted her excitedly on her return.

Two less adaptive patterns were noted among the other toddlers: one group—following the avoidant pattern—explored actively regardless of the mother's presence or absence and seemed to have a cool, slightly detached attitude toward their mothers; they gave observers the impression that they were somewhat mistrustful and perhaps prematurely independent. Another pattern—the ambivalent pattern—was observed among children who showed little or no exploratory behavior and were anxious about the mother's absence but ambivalent on her return. These two less adaptive patterns seemed to signal later behavior problems, and longer term studies on children up to kindergarten age did show that the securely attached children continue to do much better than the avoidant or ambivalent children.

In previous home observations, the mothers had been rated on several scales (acceptance, cooperation, sensitivity to the baby's signals). It turned out, not surprisingly, that mothers of the attached group—the children who were unambivalent toward their mothers and whose exploration partly depended on their presence—scored much higher on these measures than did the mothers of avoidant and ambivalent children.

Research of this kind suggests that the ability to seek out change and to use it grows out of previously existing structures. This principle applies to adult development as well, except that, in adulthood, the periods of change and stability appear to alternate more slowly.

Stability and Transition in Adulthood

In *The Seasons of a Man's Life*, developmental psychologist Daniel Levinson underscores the importance of stability by introducing as his major analytic tool the concept of "the life structure." He defines the life structure as "the basic pattern or design of a person's life at a given time." The life structure, he says, is the product of choices an individual has made in terms of love relationships, occupation, marriage and the family, use of solitude, and social roles—in other words, the risks he or she has taken or avoided. At any given time, these components can be described for a particular individual, and their relative importance can be charted. Periods of laying down a life structure—making choices that will determine the quality and importance of the components—are followed by periods of destroying that structure and laying down a new one.

Transition, says Levinson, means leaving Structure A—severing relations with it, so to speak—and moving toward a new structure that is as yet unborn. The transition periods are times of disequilibrium and anxiety. But dangers arise both in moving and in staying put. If we stay with a structure after we have outgrown it, we may betray ourselves and limit our possibilties; if we break out, we impose burdens on ourselves and may fail to find what we seek. Either way there are dangers and losses as well as gains.

When Levinson says that almost half our adult life is spent in remaking that life, he emphasizes the need to redefine ourselves at these transition phases, the need to rethink and resolve such crucial polarities as young versus old, masculine versus feminine, destruction versus creation, attachment versus separation. For each of the oppositions, we need to honor both poles and to develop a balance, but the balance shifts for each of us at different points in our lives. (In the masculine-feminine dimension, for example, research shows that a greater androgyny appears to develop with age—older men becoming "softer" than they were in midlife, older women becoming more "assertive"— each sex moving toward the contrasexual pole).

Every initiation is also a termination of what came before. The structure-building periods are necessary for stability; the structure-changing periods are necessary for growth. This process represents the overriding polarity we must integrate in our lives: the polarity of change versus continuity, the problem of how to maintain a continuous sense of ourselves while growing.

It is interesting, in the light of the now fashionable emphasis on transitions, transformations, and passages, that Levinson takes the view that the stable structure is *at least* as important as the transition. If our lives were nothing but transitions, we would feel as though we were being whirled in a centrifuge. But if they were nothing but stable structures, we would experience ourselves as inert lumps. At the one pole, we risk anxiety; at the other, depression. And our lives must seek to veer between the two as we try to combine solidity with forward movement, security with risk.

Part II
OF RISKS
AND RISK TAKERS

Chapter 3
Styles of Making
Risky Decisions

> Just as the bride's mother may weep at a wedding, what
> is a love story for one may mean bereavement for another.
> Even the bridegroom, by convention, holds a wake for his
> bachelor days on the eve of his marriage. Change appears
> as fulfillment or loss to different people, and to the same
> person at different times.
>
> Peter Marris, *Loss and Change*

In Chapter 2 we looked at risk as part of our larger experience of change—the inevitability of change, the increasing pace of change in our time, and the price we pay for change. We also noted the limits of our tolerance for change and the need for a model of change within structure.

Now I want to focus on an aspect of risk taking that is more immediate and more personal: How do people go about making risky decisions? This chapter aims to do three things:

to alert you, the reader, to various parts of the decision-making process;
to give you a chance to assess your own approach to making major life
decisions; and
finally, to set out a model of three decision-making styles.

These styles are part of risk-taking behavior because they have to do with the way people go about making the major life decisions that are big risks. I will have occasion to refer to these styles often in the rest of the book, both in the case-history examples and in our exploration of the risk-taking process.

ASSESSING YOUR APPROACH TO RISKY DECISIONS

Dimensions of the Decision-making Process

In order to prepare yourself for Self-Assessment Exercise 1, you need to have some idea of the components of the decision-making process.

The first dimension is a general attitude of temperamental preference, which could be labeled caution versus daring. It has to do with how much we seek out new stimuli and how much we cling to the old, known ones. This *attitude toward change* is very important in determining the number and nature of the risks you will take. A cautious person will require a much greater degree of discomfort with circumstances to initiate change than a daring person would require. What might represent comfortable familiarity to one might mean utter boredom to the other.

Once you are confronted with the need to take a major risk that involves a series of important decisions, you may respond to the challenge in a number of different ways. In looking for various alternatives, what is your *search strategy*? Do you provide yourself with a large range of choices, or do you typically focus on only one or two? Do you note the pluses and minuses of each choice, or do you have a built-in bias, noting only the advantages or only the drawbacks?

How big a part do your *feelings* play in your ultimate decision? Some people tend to rule them out as irrelevant and distracting; others appear to rely on them almost exclusively, operating on hunch and intuition. Still others deliberately weigh their feelings and use them as part of the equation.

Do you have an implicit *decision rule* about how good or "right" any choice you make must be? In other words, do you feel that there is a perfect decision out there that you must struggle to unearth? Or, on the contrary, do you believe that almost any decision you make will be good enough? And how loose or tight is your judgment of "good enough"? Does it mean "any notion that really takes my fancy" or something that requires some pondering and self-scrutiny?

How strong is your *sense of consequence*, and what flavor does it have? How much do you think ahead to the outcome of your action—just to the immediate future, or beyond that? Do you tend to ignore consequences and to assume that you can improvise as the need arises, since everything usually works out for the best? Do you have the opposite view—that nothing usually works out, so you have to prepare for calamity? Do you anticipate that good as well as bad things flow from almost every major choice, and do you make an attempt to see what those consequences will be?

These basic feelings of optimism (sometimes reasonable, sometimes blind) or pessimism (sometimes justified, sometimes exaggerated) are bound to enter into the anticipatory feelings with which we approach a big step. Are your *predecision emotions* mostly feelings of pleasure and excitement, mostly fears of possible misfortune, or mostly mixed, with some attention to both? Do you experience ambivalence in such cases—strong mixed feelings? If so, can you tolerate that mixture and go on to resolve it, or are you incapacitated by the conflict?

How thorough are you in thinking through the alternatives, and how much *time and effort* do you expend in coming to a major decision? Do you keep looking for alternatives long after most people would have said, "Enough!"; or do you short-circuit your search because you can't tolerate the uncertainty of mulling over possibilities—and so end up grabbing for the first likely possibility?

Once you have come close to making a major decision, how do you approach *new information* on the subject? Are you still able to consider it, or do you quickly rule it out as making the choice too complicated? Are you open to relevant new information, or do you shut it out? Some people not only are open to new input but almost feel compelled to keep tracking it down, even after coming close to a decision. Is that how you function?

Having made a decision to take a big step, what is your *postdecision behavior*? Do you just plunge into action without reconsidering? Do you often feel you're about to make a mistake and seek to change the decision? Or do you try, after reasonable pondering, to bolster your decision so that you will be able to act on it with confidence?

Finally, when the risky decision has been made and acted on and the entire process of taking a risk is completed, what happens? Do you make any attempt to *evaluate* the entire sequence you've been through—the process and its consequences? Or do you not seek to weigh what has happened and what it means to you? If you do evaluate the risk, how do you do it: by blaming yourself for things that haven't worked out or by seeing what you can learn from the experience—from the failures as well as the successes?

These dimensions, which are suggestive, not exhaustive,* are reflected in the ten items of the self-assessment exercise that follows.

---

*The reader who wishes to learn more about steps in the decision-making process can consult Irving L. Janis and Leon Mann, *Decision Making: A Psychological Analysis of Conflict, Choice, and Commitment*, which is a review and integration of work from both the clinic and the laboratory; and Daniel T. Wheeler and Irving L. Janis, *A Practical Guide for Making Decisions*, which is a more pragmatic guide and is addressed to a more general audience.

Self-Assessment Exercise 1: How Do You Make Risky Decisions?

Although people rarely are completely consistent in their decision-making styles, most of us can detect some regularity in the way we make *important* decisions. Think of the important life decisions you have made (e.g., marriage, divorce, major moves, career changes), and then answer the following questions. You may not be able to answer some with complete confidence, but give the answers that come closest to what you believe. This is *not* a test; it is just a device to help you understand your own decision-making behavior. For each dimension, choose the one response out of three that best describes how you usually respond in making a big decision.

DIMENSION

                                           ITEMS

    I. Attitude toward change

        ____(1) I prefer security to novelty.

        ____(2) I value security and novelty about equally.

        ____(3) I prefer novelty to security.

    II. Search strategy

        ____(1) I make a quick overall survey of possibilities, hoping that something will hit me.

        ____(2) I keep producing and then going over my possible choices.

        ____(3) I think of a number of alternatives but stop after reasonable search.

    III. Attention to feelings

        ____(1) I decide among alternatives not only by reasoning but by taking my feelings into account.

        ____(2) I make major decisions almost exclusively on the basis of my feelings.

        ____(3) I mistrust my feelings as a basis for a major decision; I try to use reason almost entirely.

    IV. Decision rule

        ____(1) I believe there is one right decision, and it's my job to dig it out.

_____(2) I believe there is no one right decision; I just need to find one that is good enough.

_____(3) I believe in choosing the first decision that really grabs me.

V. Sense of consequence

_____(1) I don't try to predict consequences of my decision because I just expect things will work out okay.

_____(2) I do think about consequences, tending to focus on the bad things that might happen.

_____(3) I try to think of both the good and bad consequences of my decision.

VI. Predecision emotions

_____(1) In thinking about taking a risky step I feel mostly anxiety.

_____(2) In thinking about taking a risky step, I feel a mixture of anxiety and excitement.

_____(3) In thinking about taking a risky step, I feel mostly excitement.

VII. Time expended in decision-making process

_____(1) I usually make decisions—even big ones—quickly.

_____(2) I usually take a fairly long time to make big decisions.

_____(3) I usually take a very long time to make big decisions.

VIII. Attitude toward new information

_____(1) I will consider new information even after I've arrived at a probable decision.

_____(2) I'm not interested in getting new information after · I've made a probable decision.

_____(3) I feel compelled either to seek out new information or to shut it out after I've made a probable decision.

IX. Postdecision strategy

_____(1) Once I've made a decision, I usually don't think about it before launching into action.

_____(2) Once I've made a decision, I often experience serious doubts and may change my mind.

_____(3) Once I've made a decision, I usually rally behind it after rechecking.

X. Evaluating the outcome of a risky decision

_____(1) After I have acted on the decision, I tend to worry or regret that I didn't do something else

_____(2) After I have acted on the decision, I tend to put it out of my mind.

_____(3) After I have acted on the decision, I tend to think about what I have learned from it.

Scoring the Risky Decision Exercise

Table 3 (see pages 56–57) contains a rearrangement of the items from the risky decision exercise you have just completed. The table has two purposes.

First, if you read down the columns of the table, you will get a quick idea of the three basic risk-taking styles to be discussed in the rest of this chapter. I call these styles the anxious (Style A), the balanced (Style B), and the careless (Style C).

Anxious risk takers make big decisions with great effort, indecision, and fear of making mistakes. They take a great deal of time and tend to ruminate and worry about the outcome. Balanced risk takers make big decisions fairly slowly and are more concerned with reasonably good outcomes than with fear of failure or the need to make a perfect decision. They tend to plan and to review but without worrying a great deal. Careless risk takers make big decisions quickly, with little experience of mixed feelings; they may feel inappropriately optimistic, and they tend to spend little time in introspection or evaluation. Very few people are all A, all B, or all C. Most of us are mixtures, with a primary weighting on Style B.

To get a picture of your own style in making risky decisions, you can use the table to score your responses to the exercise. The number of each exercise response item is given in parentheses. Reading across for each dimension, simply circle the number that corresponds to your response. For example, if you checked response (2) under Dimension II, Search strategy ("I keep producing and then going over my possible choices"), you would circle that response in the Style A column of the table.

When you have finished circling the responses for all ten dimensions, tally the total numbers of A responses, B responses, and C responses. This will give you an idea of the relative balance of the three styles within your personality. You can then compare your pattern with that of others who have taken this questionnaire in workshops on risk and change (described in the next section, "What Your Response Pattern Means").

It might also be interesting to have someone who knows you very well also rate you on the exercise items to see how your self-assessment meshes with someone else's perception of your decision-making style.

What Your Response Pattern Means

Now that you have some idea of your pattern of responses to the risky decision exercise, you may still be wondering what that pattern means. There are two ways of making your response pattern more intelligible. One is to compare yourself with others who have taken the same exercise. In my sample of 294 people in career change and risk workshops, the average number of Style A responses was 6.7; the average number of B responses was 2.3; and the average number of C responses was 1.0. Although a few individuals responded as balanced risk takers in all ten dimensions, most people showed a mixture. Since these workshop participants tended to be fairly cautious people, many of them schoolteachers, there were more A than C responses, as we would expect.

The goal is to be as balanced in your decision making and risk taking as possible, without expecting perfection. By being aware of the ways in which you are more like an A or more like a C you can sometimes work to reduce these tendencies a little. This is hard, because our style is so deeply a part of ourselves. But sometimes we can learn to allow or correct for it. A highly worrisome person can learn to tell herself, "Hey wait a minute... I'm trying to make the perfect decision again, and that's not possible." A very impulsive person may be able to say to himself, "It's not my style, but I guess I should take a while to let this decision sit before I act on it." I will point out further examples of allowing for or correcting for style as we go along.

A second way to understand your style is to see how it might look in relation to the extremes, as these are illustrated in the examples on pages 58–61.

Table 3 STYLES OF MAKING RISKY DECISIONS

DIMENSION	STYLE A (THE ANXIOUS RISK TAKER)	STYLE B (THE BALANCED RISK TAKER)	STYLE C (THE CARELESS RISK TAKER)
I. Attitude toward change	Prefers security to novelty (1)	Values security and novelty about equally (2)	Prefers novelty to security (3)
II. Search strategy	Keeps producing and then going over possible choices (2)	Thinks of a number of alternatives but stops after reasonable search (3)	Makes a quick overall survey of possibilities, hoping something will hit him/her (1)
III. Attention to feelings	Mistrusts feelings as basis for making major decision; tries to use reason almost entirely (3)	Decides among alternatives not only by reasoning but by taking feelings into account (1)	Makes major decisions almost exclusively on the basis of feelings (2)
IV. Decision rule	Believes there is one right decision and it's his/her job to dig it out (1)	Believes there is no one right decision; just needs to find one that is good enough (2)	Believes in choosing the first decision that really grabs him/her (3)
V. Sense of consequence	Thinks about consequences, tending to focus on the bad things that might happen (2)	Tries to think of both the good and bad consequences of the decision (3)	Doesn't try to predict consequences because expects things will work out okay (1)
VI. Predecision emotions	Feels mostly anxiety (1)	Feels mixture of anxiety and excitement (2)	Feels mostly excitement (3)

	A	B	C
VII. Time expended in decision-making process	Takes very long time to make big decisions (3)	Takes fairly long time to make big decisions (2)	Makes even big decisions quickly (1)
VIII. Attitude toward new information	Feels compelled either to seek out new information or to shut it out after making probable decision (3)	Will consider new information even after arriving at probable decision (1)	Is not interested in getting new information after making probable decision (2)
IX. Postdecision strategy	Having made decision, often experiences serious doubts and may change his/her mind (2)	Having made decision, usually rallies behind it after rechecking (3)	Having made decision, usually doesn't think about it before launching into action (1)
X. Evaluating the outcome of a risky decision	After acting on the decision, tends to worry or regret not doing something else (1)	After acting on the decision, tends to think about what has been learned from it (3)	After acting on the decision, tends to put it out of his/her mind (2)
	Total number of A responses ____	Total number of B responses ____	Total number of C responses ____

Numbers in parentheses refer to item numbers on Self-Assessment Exercise 1.

EXAMPLES OF RISK-TAKING STYLES

I want to look more closely now at the anxious and the careless risk takers, Style A and Style C. (Style B will occupy us for most of the next two chapters.) I want to emphasize that in the descriptions that follow, I am creating a composite of a number of details from actual people who are "more or less" that way. Alan and Carolyn can be taken as prototypes whose characteristics are exaggerated for emphasis and clarity. As Count Alfred Korzybski, the Polish philosopher, wrote, "The map is not the territory." A map simplifies, condenses, and focuses what is more bumpy and diffuse in the real world. With this caution in mind, then, let's look at some hypothetical examples.

Alan, An Anxious Risk Taker (Style A)

Alan, a 30-year-old unmarried computer analyst, has taken very few risks in his life. He went to the local university for his B.A. in mathematics and enrolled in the doctoral program of the same university, spending seven years as a graduate student while he supported himself as a research assistant and occasional consultant. After trying unsuccessfully for years to write his dissertation, he decided to give up on it, and two years ago, he quit school. He already had a good job as a computer analyst waiting for him.

In his life outside of work, Alan has had a long-term relationship with a woman and has lived with her for the past three years. Although she is pressing for marriage, he cannot quite bring himself to take the step. He is sure they "probably will marry at some point," but the time never seems to be quite right.

Alan is witty in an ironic way and highly intelligent; more noticeable about him than these qualities, however, is the intense, effortful activity he brings to everything he does, whether at work or at "play," building model ships as a hobby.

Alan finds making decisions—even the smallest ones—agonizingly difficult. His most recent problem was to decide whether to change jobs from the firm he had been working at for the past three years to another, at better pay and with somewhat more responsibility; taking the second job meant either moving or spending a much longer time commuting, both of which he was reluctant to do.

Whenever Alan has to make a decision, he draws up a careful balance sheet of the pluses and minuses for each alternative. But it is hard for him to act on his guidelines, because as soon as he thinks of a "plus" about one of the options, a "minus" about that alternative comes to mind. It is as though he has to undo every step he takes in one direction by taking a step in the opposite direction.

Similarly, when, after much effort and vacillation, he has finally made a decision, he often experiences persistent doubt and seeks to change it. He had decided, for example, based on his balance sheet, to move to a different section within the first company rather than to change firms. But no sooner did he announce the decision to his boss than he "knew" it was the "wrong" one. (The frequent quotation marks I feel it necessary to use in describing Alan suggest the forced or arbitrary quality of much that he thinks and does.) Alan firmly believes that there is "one right decision" in every choice problem and that his task, through concentrated unwavering effort, is to discover it or, more accurately, to pry it out. Although he deplores his indecisiveness, he actually prefers hovering, hummingbirdlike, in a state of indecision, to settling on an alternative, because being in the middle means he has not yet incurred the overwhelming risk of committing himself to "the wrong choice."

As you might imagine, Alan is very afraid to trust his hunches. In fact, much of his life has been spent training himself more or less systematically not to have hunches. Brilliantly efficient in his work, he is nevertheless rather concrete and literal-minded. He believes his feelings are very poor guides in making major moves, and, indeed, he frequently rejects his own feelings on the grounds that it is not "rational" to feel such-and-such (anger at his boss, pleasure at small accomplishments, tenderness toward his girlfriend, sadness at his inability to finish his degree). Because he believes that feelings, like thoughts and ideas, ought to be "rational," whenever they aren't—that is, almost always—he berates himself for feeling something he should not. In fact, his behavior tends to be governed most of the time by "shoulds" rather than by felt wishes. He mistrusts his wishes as irrational, and this gives his "shoulds" a harsh, arbitrary force, simply because they are so disconnected from his needs.

Someone of this sort, as psychologist David Shapiro has put it so well, can be seen to "exert more or less continuous pressure on himself while at the same time working under the strain of that pressure." Alan is thus both his own overseer and the slave of that overseer. Metaphorical stopwatch in hand, he sets deadlines for himself that are often quite arbitrary. Moreover, he does not recognize either how arbitrary they are or how self-imposed; the deadlines actually appear to come from outside himself, to be built into the nature of things. "I have to make this decision by Thursday," he will tell himself, and then will scramble frantically as though Thursday were a "real" deadline rather than a self-imposed and unrealistic one which could readily be self-*un*imposed.

In thinking about a risky decision, what Alan mainly does is worry about what could go wrong. He generally sees decisions as demanding a choice between two or more undesirable alternatives. That is, he focuses mostly on the negative consequences of any choice: "If I change firms, I'll lose the seniority I've built up in my company. But if I stay, I'll have to do the same boring work I've done for the last three years." Ths is how he presents choices to himself. Without distortion, the same pair of alternatives could have been stated, equally accurately, as "If I stay, I'll continue my seniority. If I change, I'll have new learning opportunities." It's the old question of whether a glass is half-empty or half-full.

When asked what worrying *does* for him, Alan finally admits that it feels like a form of action: "If I worry, I feel like I'm *doing* something about the decision." This more-or-less continuous mental activity—really only mental wheel spinning—is often a parody of thinking, designed to ward off unwanted thoughts and impulses while giving Alan the illusion that he is "accomplishing something—not just goofing off and neglecting the decision." He equates worrying with fruitful mental activity, like planning or problem solving. The driven quality of Alan's mental life carries over to his actions as well. When Alan is building his model ships, his frowning concentration suggests hard work rather than play.

Similarly, at a party, he often "tries to be spontaneous"—a patent contradiction. Although he seldom enjoys a truly playful moment, occasionally his girlfriend, who is good-natured and matter-of-fact, can "get him to relax." Most of the time he labors with little freedom of choice under what he feels to be crushing responsibilities—a perception that accurately reflects his submission to his harsh internal taskmaster. Concern about his "image" and a pervasive fear of failing are important motivating forces for him.

The irony is that, because Alan feels his decision-making process to be so painful and protracted, and because its outcome often seems so arbitrary (being disconnected from his real wants), he will often throttle his indecisiveness and list making by taking impulsive action. Thus, on the decision to move to the other company, he first exhausted a whole battery of "rational" considerations for and against each option; then he made a decision and reversed it; and he finally ended up flipping a coin, telling himself, "Tails I'll move, heads I'll stay." The coin came up heads, which is probably what he really wanted all along, although he had not been able to allow himself to recognize his wants *explicitly*. (If the coin had come up tails, he might have found some pretext to justify flipping it again.) Therefore, despite his elaborately—even excessively— "rational" procedure, Alan often ends up behaving like someone at the opposite end of the risk-taking spectrum, someone who is highly impulsive. This is not surprising, for, as Shapiro points out, both people like Alan and those who are the impulsive opposite suffer from a "defect of intentionality." Both types have difficulty recognizing and experiencing their own wishes and acting on them *deliberately*.

Carolyn: A Careless Risk Taker (Style C)

Carolyn can be considered to be the opposite of Alan in most ways. She is a 27-year-old woman who works as a nightclub hostess while she is trying to break into the rock music scene as a composer/singer. Tall and attractive, with long, dark hair and a brilliant smile, she wears flashy clothes, which she varies like costumes. She is alternately the sophisticated hostess, the country-western star, the punk rock hoyden, the barefoot hippie. Her tempo, unlike Alan's, is speedy: she talks fast and animatedly, and she is physically restless—twisting her hair, tapping her feet, gesturing flamboyantly.

Carolyn has done many risky things in her life. She was married at 17 to her high-school boyfriend and was divorced three years later. She has lived with several men, the latest being her best friend—a gay guitar player—for two years. She has had two abortions. She worked in a gambling casino for eight months. She is talented and regards herself as serious about her music, but she is also easily distractible. She started studying fashion design, quit after a year and a half, but thinks she may return to it some day. She once "dropped everything" for a sudden opportunity to ride across the country with a friend who was going to New York. She was in and out of the drug scene in the 1970s, "doing speed, mostly." She is attractive, makes friends easily, and can be very generous.

Carolyn often experiences herself as "being seized" by an impulse or whim, and she may make a major decision in just that way. Two years ago, for example, with a loan from her parents, she bought a house. What she did was look at three houses, decide the last one was just fine, and make a bid on the spot. "It just felt right," she said. She hates to deliberate over decisions; unlike Alan, who drags out the predecision period as long as possible, she often reduces the pain of ambiguity by making snap decisions. Occasionally, these decisions turn out to be good, intuitive moves. Often, however, they turn out to be foolhardy. She discovered after having bought her house, for example, that it had some severe structural flaws she hadn't noticed on her quick inspection; there was almost no closet space, and the roof leaked. But it's hard for her to learn from this experience to be more deliberate. In general, her strategy is to plunge in and to take care of problems as they come up rather than anticipating them. She actually prides herself on "being a gambler" and being daring, and she seems to need to function that way across the board.

In immediate, short-range decisions, Carolyn can be efficient and purposeful. In auditioning last year, she quickly but thoroughly weeded out the agents who might not be useful, found the best one in Los Angeles, and signed up with her. She is generally confident and excited about the decisions she makes, even though she frequently has found that her choice has had "unexpected" consequences.

Literally a gambler during the period she worked at a casino in Las Vegas, she has almost always acted on her hunches. As opposed to Alan, with his effortful concentration and worry, Carolyn goes about her life with an air of insouciance. What grabs her is usually what she does. Choice for her is not the convoluted labyrinth it is for Alan. It is a river, and she tends to "go with the flow."

Paradoxically, despite all her activity and movement, her decision process is actually rather passive, depending heavily on impulse and external cues or pressures. Like Alan, she seems to be unaware of deep or continuous wants or of willing a course of action in a sustained and significant way. The rapidity of her decision making sometimes works in her favor, but more often it suggests her discomfort in examining her motives and in dealing with uncertainty and ambiguity. Despite her careless and easygoing facade, Carolyn often seems to be driven by forces outside her awareness or control.

The Balanced Risk Taker (Style B)

If Alan represents a too-constricted, anxious risk taker, and Carolyn a too-impulsive, careless risk taker, what would a more moderate style look like? A balanced risk taker would be someone who could sometimes opt for major change and sometimes choose to stay put; someone who could spend a fair amount of time considering alternatives but would not consider such a list more "binding" than certain internal cues about feelings; someone who could tolerate the ambiguity of not deciding but could also move into action after reasonable deliberation; someone who could plan fail-safe measures if the consequences of a major decision didn't turn out as hoped; someone who neither refuses to reflect on a risk that has been taken nor uses that risk for self-recrimination but takes, instead, the instrumental stance of asking what can be learned from such a move.

In order to emphasize that balanced risk takers are not unreal paragons, outside our knowledge or experience, I will present in the next chapter the case histories of six adults who have struggled successfully—and in differing ways—to master major risks. It is important to realize that there are a number of *variants* of effective risk-taking styles, ranging from the slightly more cautious to the slightly more impetuous. No one is a perfect risk taker any more than he or she is a perfect mate, a perfect money manager, a perfect parent. Most of us fall in the midrange somewhere, and it is for people in this midrange that this book is primarily designed, since extreme styles such as Alan's or Carolyn's are difficult to modify through a book or through didactic instruction. (Carolyn would probably be too restless to read such a book, and Alan would want more "rules" than I would be prepared to give.)

To repeat, most of us *are* in the large middle area—fairly balanced risk takers, with a smattering of Alan-like qualities and a few of Carolyn's. Thus, a woman who is slow to take a major risk may be a plunger in one area of her life, such as playing the horses or buying real estate. A man who operates largely on hunches may be able through self-discipline to force himself to spell out the consequences of a really major change before taking action. Some such inconsistencies are both inevitable and healthy. In fact, several studies have shown that *extreme consistency* of risk-taking style across the board may actually indicate "motivational disturbance."

EXTREMISM AND CONSISTENCY IN RISK-TAKING BEHAVIOR: RESEARCH FINDINGS

A considerable body of theory and research stemming from the studies of psychologist John Atkinson and his co-workers suggests that people who have a high *need for achievement* tend to be moderate risk takers, while those who are motivated more strongly by a *need to avoid failure* prefer either very risky or very safe choices in chance tasks. The cautious preference among those who want to avoid failure makes obvious sense; the risky preference needs explaining. It may be that when you are very afraid of failing, choosing a risky task at which *most* people fail will reduce your own anxiety in this regard.

Thus, in a study by C. H. Mahone, students with a high need to avoid failure were found to choose occupations that were too difficult or too easy for their ability level. Similarly, Eugene Burnstein noted that, although subjects with a high fear of failure were willing to settle for less prestigious occupations than were subjects with a high need for achievement, they were also much more likely to consider that they might hold such exalted positions as Supreme Court justice, diplomat, or state governor. This evidence on under- and over-aspiration parallels some laboratory evidence cited by Kogan and Wallach—that subjects who are anxious about failing make extremely high- or low-risk choices.

An important related issue has to do with the generality or consistency of a person's risk-taking style. In their laboratory research, Kogan and Wallach correlated risk-taking behavior with two personality traits. One (based on a measure of anxiety about taking tests) they labeled "fear of failure"; the other (based on a measure of the need to maintain a good image) they called "defensiveness."

Subjects who were secure—that is, those who scored low both on fear of failure and on defensiveness—tended to *vary* their risk-taking stance, depending on the situation. When they found they weren't winning on a betting task, they tended to express dissatisfaction with their strategy and to modify it. On a final, double-or-nothing bet in which everything was staked on a single roll of the dice, they tended to risk if their winnings had been low but to adopt a more conservative strategy if their winnings had been high. In other words, they took into account environmental contingencies, context, rationality, and, perhaps most important, what they had to lose.

The less secure subjects—those who scored high on fear of failure and high on defensiveness—tended to respond much more consistently. Some were always daring and some were always cautious, no matter what conditions prevailed. If they amassed small winnings, they didn't express dissatisfaction but instead persisted even more doggedly in their preferred strategy. On the double-or-nothing final roll of the dice, they again behaved exactly as they had behaved when the risks and payoffs were different. They seemed to have a rigid, automatic decision rule that governed their risk-taking behavior. For some it was "Always play it safe." For others, it was "Always play it risky." This internal rule appeared to take precedence over the realistic demands of the situation. We will look more closely at people who operate from simple, binding decision rules when, in Chapter 6 we meet Meredith—a woman who couldn't risk—and Paul—a man who had to risk.

To conclude our survey of risk-taking styles, we can see that the balanced risk taker is most importantly a flexible risk taker who can modify his or her behavior depending on the feedback from the environment, the effects on others, and the effect on her- or himself. The Style B risk taker also considers the *centrality* of the decision; he or she will invest far less energy in choosing a belt than in choosing a mate. By contrast, the Style A risk taker may treat both as equally major, whereas the Style C risk taker may treat both as equally insignificant.

Most of us are not pure cases. We are a little anxious about failure and we have some need to "look good," but basically we are supple enough so that these concerns are not overriding. Fallible as we are, we can accept our fallibility. We can make mistakes and recoup and learn from them as well as from our successes.

The next chapter presents the stories of six people who did just that— initiated major life changes and learned from their risks.

Chapter 4
Models for Risk Taking:
Interpersonal Risks

In the previous chapter, we looked at styles of risk taking, describing the major types as the anxious (Style A), the balanced (Style B), and the careless (Style C) risk taker. In the next two chapters, we will follow six actual people as they describe major changes they have made. I interviewed these people at length and gave them the exercise on risky decision making included in Chapter 3. All of them were basically Style B—that is, most of their responses were scored as B, with slightly different balances of the occasional A and C responses. Thus, some move into their major risks with a more cautious, more deliberative style and are more worry-prone; others are more decisive and slightly more impulsive. But all of them are reasonably flexible, thoughtful, articulate people who can introspect and can reflect on what went on as they made the kinds of changes most of us face at some time in our lives.

These six men and women are basically ordinary people—neither impaired nor heroic in their experiences or capacities. But even ordinary people can have extraordinary moments of passion and illumination. In his introduction to *Creatures of Circumstance*, W. Somerset Maugham quotes Chekhov as saying, "People do not go to the North Pole and fall off icebergs.

They go to the office, quarrel with their wives, and eat cabbage soup." In rebuttal, Maugham writes, "But people do go to the North Pole, and if they don't fall off icebergs they undergo experiences as perilous." The next two chapters tell the stories of six people who at some points in their lives have undergone perilous experiences and have grown from them.

The risks we will be looking at are the crucial and distinctive ones in our era of rapidly accelerating change and shifting values: deciding to have or not to have a child as the safe years for childbearing begin to run out; getting a divorce after a long marriage; uprooting oneself from one part of the country to another; changing from one career to a considerably different one, while trying to integrate what is useful from previous work experience.

This chapter focuses on interpersonal risks, in which a major issue is how to balance our own needs and feelings with those of others who are vitally affected by our decisions. The next chapter examines geographical moves and career changes, which test our ability to maintain a sense of continuity in the midst of disruptions of our physical surroundings and work life.

Each case is followed by some conclusions about what that person's experience can tell us about risk taking. Names and identifying details have been changed, of course, to insure confidentiality.

CASE HISTORIES

Jenny and Bob: Having a Child at 35

"Only when you pair off do you get enough feedback to know what you're about."

Having a child, the decision Jenny and Bob confronted, is a simple decision in terms of the number of alternatives; the choices are only yes or no (with adoption as a possible third alternative under yes). But it's also a very weighty decision, and its effects are irreversible. Furthermore, *consciously* deciding to have a child or not is usually a joint decision, and that raises special concerns. We will look at the special difficulties in a joint decision as opposed to an individually made decision—particularly at how two people with very different styles and separate agendas can come to agree on a common choice that is emotionally weighted for both. Other issues include the physical and psychological concerns in having a child in one's thirties, ways of preparing for making such a decision, and the real and imagined losses and gains.

* * *

On Jenny and Bob Bigelow's mailbox, there's a plastic label with their name on it; underneath is a second label that says "Erin." Erin, it turns out, is their delicate-featured, cheerful, curious, eight-month-old daughter. How Jenny and Bob decided to have her is a story of the sort many older parents are living through these days, as women who have been putting off children come up against the louder tick of their biological clocks.

I interviewed Jenny and Bob in their apartment in Ann Arbor, Michigan, while Erin was amusing herself in her playpen—intermittently turning on her cradle-gym music box, rolling, and babbling—and later being held by her parents.

Jenny—small, dark-haired, energetic, intense—met Bob seven years ago at a yoga center in Chicago, where she was meditating and he was doing T'ai Chi Ch'uan. Bob, a graduate student in public health at the University of Michigan, had come to Chicago for a weekend visit. Jenny did special education with disabled children in Chicago, after having been an airline stewardess and flight supervisor for Pan Am.

From the first minute Jenny saw Bob, she was drawn to his handsome, delicate face. "When we talked," she says, "I could see that he was a sensitive, caring man, not like anyone I'd ever known—low-key, vulnerable, very—" she gropes for the word,"—very spiritual." After seven months of traveling between Chicago and Ann Arbor, she began to live with Bob in his one-room apartment.

Warm and gregarious, Jenny has many Style C characteristics: she loves excitement and movement, acting impulsively, traveling to new places on no notice. That was part of the appeal of being a stewardess. But she came to question her own style: "I realized it had been a great escape. I could get on an airplane and could fly away every time I had a problem. You don't have to make a commitment to anything because you know it will be interrupted."

Jenny was 29 when she met Bob; he was 31. At that point, she no longer expected to get married. She had been engaged and had lived with a man, but these relationships had ended, and she had begun to believe she would not find anyone she would want to share her life with. She didn't think about children because the idea of being a single mother did not seem workable. She desperately *wanted* to get married, but she didn't believe it would happen.

When she met Bob she knew from the beginning that "this was going to be special." They lived together for a year and a half—Bob resisting marriage, Jenny pressing for it. As Jenny explains:

> It didn't have anything to do with children. I have this family tape in my head that says you're no one till you get married. It's not rational, but that's how it is with me. I've always thought: college, graduate school, get married. Children didn't really enter into that scenario somehow. It was the traditional thing about women getting married—like this 1940s book I found in a rummage sale. It's written for little girls to tell them what they can do when they grow up. It says, "You can be a bride." As though that were a career, you know, right in there with being a ballerina.

Jenny prevailed, but she did give up her wish for a big church wedding in deference to Bob's wish to have an outdoor ceremony in a local glen. And so they were married; the bride was 31, the groom, 33.

The early years of their marriage were good ones. Jenny got a full-time job working in the university's public information department. Bob plugged along, the perennial graduate student on research assistantships. He never quite got to writing his dissertation, but he had a chance to do interesting, worthwhile work—a brief stint on a maternal and child health project in Nigeria, an internship on a program working with the terminally ill (a project Jenny joined as a part-time volunteer). They had a close, trusting marriage. The main question was when Bob would get his Ph.D., but that didn't seem urgent. Neither did having a family—at least for the first two years.

When Jenny turned 33, however, she began to get increasingly anxious, feeling that, if she was going to have a child, she should do it before she reached 35.

How did they deal with it? Bob—now holding Erin—smiles and says, "What do you do when you've spent most of your adult life around universities? You take a course." In this case it was a six-week workshop, "Considering Parenthood," led by a talented young social worker who had had years of experience helping couples think through decisions about pregnancy, childbearing, and childrearing.

In the course of the workshop, and with the support of others in the group, the participants clarified the main issues for themselves. They were surprised to discover that, although all of them shared many concerns, each person had a slightly different focus.

For Jenny, as for many of the other women in the group, the key surface issue was what she calls "home management." She felt by now that having a child was a not-to-be-missed life experience, but she was concerned about how much responsibility she would have to shoulder for the child's care and for the continued maintenance of their quarters. All around her Jenny had seen women working and also taking on the major share of the care for infant and home, and she didn't want that to happen to her. (When I asked them what system they had used previously in dealing with the "home management" issue, Bob quipped, "An adversarial system," and they both laughed.) What Jenny and Bob worked out was not a rigid definition of rules or roles but a substantive agreement that if they had a child, they would share emotionally and physically in its care and that Jenny wouldn't have to take on total responsibility—a prospect she found not only inequitable but frightening.

(As it has worked out, they do divide responsibility more or less equally. But Jenny emphasizes that it's not the actual time but the spirit that counts. "I need to hear Bob say he's right in there to offer his support," Jenny says. "His being appreciative of what I do and offering to help—even if I don't take him up on it—makes me feel good." Bob adds that, if he "fades off" on his responsibility, the history of their agreement gets reintroduced by Jenny. Then, after reworking things for a day or so, "we go back to the arrangement.")

The other issue Jenny had to face was a psychological one: Could she be a good mother after having experienced great difficulty in her relationship with her own mother? She has had innumerable abrasive and painful encounters with her mother over the years, more of them since her father died ten years ago. She read *My Mother, Myself* three times and has spent the last few years, as she puts it, trying to "mother myself"—to give herself the nurturance she feels she didn't get from her mother. Paradoxically, this self-nurturance often occurs when she is playing with Erin: "I'm aware of our separateness, but in playing with her, it's almost like I'm a child again, playing with *me*."

Jenny describes her mother as a strong, managerial woman whose relationship with her husband took priority over her relationship with her two children. She raised Jenny as though she were her student—didactically and rationally, but without much show of affection or much emotional support. ("Even on my wedding day, I had to *ask* her if I looked pretty.")

> As a kid, I repeatedly heard her say to me, "I hope you have a child just like you." And it wasn't said as a compliment. She meant, "I hope you have a child who is as demanding, as active, as difficult as you are for me." I've worried about my mother's wish coming true, and didn't know if I could deal with a child like that. It scared me.

In spite of her fears, however, Jenny felt that having a child would be deeply fulfilling. She also hoped that being a parent would propel Bob out of his perennial graduate-student status and force him to get a job. The very qualities that had so attracted Jenny to Bob—his gentleness, his patience, his calmness—kept him able to tolerate very slow advancement toward his degree. Jenny has some Style C characteristics: she is a mover who, at one period in her life, moved 13 times in seven years; Bob's "stillness," while it was the perfect complement, could also be an irritant to her.

What were the issues for Bob? For him the problem was a different risk—not of the biological timetable or of dividing up chores but of setting personal and professional priorities. As a "professional graduate student" he was comfortable and secure. Having a child meant he would have to make decisions: Was he going to finish the dissertation and, if so, how much effort and time would that take? What would he do about getting a job once he was off the university stipend? Would they be buying a house? What kind of income would he be bringing home? What would the decision to have a child do to all these other decisions? Was it irresponsible to bring a child into the world when he was just about to enter a somewhat uncertain job market? He recalls:

> For me, having children was always one of these things you thought you would do "one of these days." *I* didn't have a biological time clock, and I'd have been willing to adopt a child, though Jenny wasn't.
> Ultimately, what the question boiled down to for me was what would I be missing by *not* having a child. Of course, if we didn't have one, I wouldn't know what I'd missed. But I was sure it would be something important. It was like standing in front of a closed door, and I felt that if I walked away from that door and then looked far, far back at it twenty years from now, I'd be sure I missed something essential.
> I didn't want to be in the position of having had a life cycle that felt—well, foreshortened. I wanted to have one that mirrored my own parents'—not in its substance but in its completeness—with *me* as the parent, trying to reinvent the life cycle for myself.

This notion brought problems because, like Jenny vis-à-vis her mother, Bob felt that his father was not a good model for the kind of father *he* would want to be. Bob had been raised essentially by his mother, because his father, though physically present, was psychologically remote. He was a good breadwinner, who helped in the external maintenance of the house and yard and, from behind his ubiquitous newspaper, delivered such truisms as "Whatever is worth doing is worth doing well." Bob had experienced his father as a self-righteous man who hid behind his rigid pronouncements in order to avoid any personal interaction that might threaten his male authority.

Thus, Bob was particularly afraid of raising a son and felt it would be easier to "start afresh" with a daughter. But before the sex of their child was determined by amniocentesis, and in order to prepare for the possibility of a male child, Bob actually went out and bought a fishing rod. Fishing, he felt, was something you did with a son—something he and his father had rarely done together.

Beyond these fears, Bob was afraid that a child would completely dominate his life for the next 20 years and box him into a commitment he had never really faced up to. "There seemed to be 10,000 problems," he muses, "and about three rewards." Looking back now at their first eight months with Erin, Bob says that the balance was far different from what he had imagined:

> Again I think of the door. You imagine the other side as containing a million prob-
> lems and wonder *why* anyone would go through that door. But having passed
> through the door and abandoned your list of anxieties, you see that problems be-
> come merely the things you do because you're there. They're no longer problems
> with a capital P. And the rewards, on the other hand—even though you can list
> them under only about three headings—are manifested *constantly*, which means the
> balance is much more favorable than I could have anticipated.

By the end of the workshop, Jenny and Bob felt pretty well committed to having a child within the next year or so. Since Bob had still not finished his dissertation and had no regular job, however, and since medical evidence now suggested that even 35 wasn't too dangerous an age to bear a child, the alarm on the biological clock could be set slightly later.

After thinking about the decision some more, both individually and together, Bob and Jenny tacitly let the decision go for awhile, allowing an incubation period for their decision to settle and connect with unconscious wishes. Then they just said to each other, "Oh, hell, let's *do* it." With characteristic dispatch and determination, Jenny became pregnant on their first try without contraceptives.

After they knew Jenny was pregnant, new fears began to surface: What kind of child would they have? Would it be normal? Would it be retarded? Amniocentesis revealed it would be free of a number of the usual genetic abnormalities this procedure can screen for, and that it would be a girl. (Characteristically, Bob had not wanted to know the sex, liking his presents to be "surprises," while Jenny had chosen to know, "because if anybody knows something that concerns me, *I* want to know it.")

With the birth of their child fairly imminent, Bob began to think more con-
cretely about what the presence of an infant would mean. While visiting some friends who had recently had a child, he saw that the house had been con-
verted into a giant playpen—an acre of empty wall-to-wall carpeting from which virtually all adult objects had been removed. Because Bob regards his home as a refuge, where he can retreat and feel surrounded by objects that have meaning for him—such as his collection of musical instruments—he wondered what he would do. (He now finds, he says, that he is giving things up "piecemeal" as Erin begins moving around.)

Jenny had other kinds of worries. Although she was committed to natural childbirth, she was afraid she would not be able to manage the pain as "com-
petently" as Bob would want her to; she felt compelled to make it clear both to

him and to her doctor that if she wanted anesthesia, she needed to be able to have it.

As it happened, both the position of the baby and the conformation of Jenny's pelvis required that she have the baby by Cesarean section. Bob was present for the surgery and for the initial bonding after the birth of their little girl. He held her in his arms for several hours while Jenny struggled to overcome the dulling effects of the anesthetics. She was exhausted; he was euphoric.

"It was only after I came home," Bob says, "that I realized that it was *my wife* whose abdomen was being cut open back there in the hospital. And it suddenly hit me what a generous impulse it was for her to allow someone to do that to her, for her to undergo all the pain and the risk. There were no words for that. I cried by myself, in awe."

Jenny had taken a six-month leave from her job and was able during that time to find a half-time job that would allow her to spend half-time at home with Erin. Since Bob's research assistantship was also half-time, they decided to sacrifice income so that they could each spend half of the day with Erin. They believe that this sharing has had a lot to do with their sense of fulfillment. Jenny thinks that perhaps other parents are running around so much, crowding so much else into their lives, that they can't focus on the joys of having an infant—the pleasures of playing with a child, watching it grow and respond and gradually gain a sense of mastery.

For Bob, having Erin represents a rediscovery of previously discarded assumptions, and having a family has become the center that gives meaning to other activities. "Working now isn't just for work itself, but it ties into the family. And working to support a family isn't simply a burden. It's *neat* to support a family—as corny as that may sound." He goes on in the same vein as he talks about people seeking out alternatives, trying to discover themselves in the hope of discovering meaning: "But for me that happened when I put the search for meaning into the context of the family."

An interesting by-product of having a child has been the change Jenny and Bob have noticed in themselves—each moving in complementary ways to be more like the other or more like the previously unrealized parts of themselves that so attracted each of them to the other. Jenny has become less controlling, more willing to tolerate disorder, more calm, and "more human." Bob has had to adapt to being with Erin by making better use of his days rather than working at night, when he's now too exhausted. *He* has had to take *more* control, to be more efficient and goal-oriented. "I feel more part of something right here, and that spills over, so that I feel more active and more self-confident."

Do they have some regrets? Only that they are tired a lot of the time and that there has been a certain loss of physical intimacy for the past ten months. "Part of it," says Jenny, "is getting back into my body again. But we've had time to demonstrate that we both care enough to hang in there and to keep connected in other ways." Near the end of her pregnancy, Jenny recalls, Bob gave her a sexy black nightgown. She looked at it and didn't know whether to laugh or cry. "There was no way I could get into that mood—or the nightgown!—right then. I still don't feel especially sexual, but I know that will come back."

Meanwhile, Bob is now planning to finish his dissertation by working on it full-time, which will mean some shifting of Erin's care. They have just made an offer on a duplex with another couple who have a daughter the same age, and the two couples will work out cooperative sitting arrangements.

Both Bob and Jenny talk about *the need for support* in decisions—support from the parents' group, from friends, from the couple with whom they are buying the house, and, above all, from each other.

Bob makes an analogy with T'ai Chi Ch'uan, an active form of meditation that ideally involves moving "with and against" a partner, pushing each other gently as you move:

> You're confronted quite directly with what you have to meditate on, which is how to stay centered given a very disruptive influence. It's easier to stay centered when you're isolated. But it's not until you pair off with another person that you get sufficient feedback to really know what you're about. A lot of people dancing alone delude themselves into thinking they're achieving a great energy flow, when in fact they're just dancing.... Solo dancing can be nice, but it's not apt to lead to the depth you can find by tuning into yourself *and* another person.

WHAT CAN BE LEARNED FROM JENNY AND BOB

In this story of a risk, we see two different temperaments—Jenny's, decisive, impetuous, and action-oriented; Bob's, contemplative, scholarly, slow-moving—coming up against each other. Both Jenny and Bob had their own concerns born out of their individual life histories. They had similar problems about identifying as a parent with their parent of the same sex. Both were receiving a kind of caring from their partner that neither had ever experienced before. This goodwill and respect for their complementarities made communication possible. Because each valued the differences of the other, in time each actually came to acquire some of those complementary characteristics.

In a joint risk such as this, a great deal of talking and sharing of feelings was necessary. It was also necessary to be able to express strong *ambivalence*. The move to seek both *information* and *support* in a group of people facing the same decision, under the guidance of a group leader, proved both informative and emotionally sustaining. As is typical, the period of scrutiny was followed by one of "doing nothing," or letting the nearly formed decision settle. Also typical is the experience of plunging into action ("Oh, hell, let's do it!"). Jenny and Bob didn't just drift into the decision, as many people do. After exhausting the available resources—and themselves—they gave it time to sit and then took the leap into the unknown that all major life changes ultimately demand.

After the decision to have a child was made, Bob and Jenny took advantage of a procedure (amniocentesis) that enabled them to reduce their uncertainty about producing a genetically deformed child. And Jenny insisted on maintaining her options about anesthesia and surgical intervention right up to the end.

In parenting, too, they have been able to share the burdens as well as the pleasures. What Bob and Jenny show most clearly is a mutual respect, a willingness to make certain compromises for the sake of the marriage—along with a strong-willed insistence on important values of temperament and belief that each was unwilling to compromise—and a thorough exploration of the risk of having a child in one's thirties.

Celia: A Running Start, A Midlife Divorce

"We thought the two of you were immortal."

Celia's story helps us see some of the early warning signals and main concerns in a midlife divorce. She handled this crisis with a great deal of concern for the others involved, and that consideration dictated the pace and nature of the break. In Celia, we see how a risk exists in the context of the entire emotional life of a person and in the lives of those close to her. We also see how undertaking physical risks—a relatively new frontier for women—can enhance taking psychological chances.

* * *

Celia Franklin is a 49-year-old pediatrician who lives in Westport, Connecticut, and practices in Bridgeport. She has a taut, runner's body, straight, firm features, and a cap of red-brown hair, cut like a helmet. She walks with the decisive gait of someone stripped for action, yet her clothes, in contrast, are soft and interesting: a macramé vest over a knit jersey, a long mauve skirt, boots. This contrast between the soft and the taut, between toughness and tenderness, has run through Celia's life. I interviewed her in her book-lined study, with its easy chairs, oriental rug, and fieldstone fireplace. Over tea, she told me about her recent divorce, the break-up of a 24-year marriage:

> It began, I'd say, with a long period of growing restlessness. About 7 or 8 years ago I first experienced this restlessness at work. I had worked in a hospital pediatric clinic for 18 years, because I believed in clinic work. After years of service with very little recognition and finally the appointment of a difficult and capricious department head...well, I began to think I needed something of my own.

Celia started to fantasize about setting up a private practice. She knew she would devote a large part of her practice to the low-fee patients she had seen in the clinic, but she needed the freedom from institutional battles that her own practice would give her. Four years ago she went into practice on her own in a group setting and began to see that she could make it away from "the nest"— the teaching hospital where she had spent all her working life since her residency training.

At that point, however, she could not yet see that the questions she had been asking about her work—"Is this all? Is it worth it? Have I overextended myself?"—were the questions she could, and later did, also ask about her marriage to Jim.

"Gradually," she says—and it is a word she uses often in this account—"I was building a separate life from Jim, trying to provide for myself the things my marriage wasn't providing. Perhaps the biggest part of that was my running."

When Celia talks about running, her expression lightens, she leans forward in her chair, and her gestures become more expansive. Running indeed seems to have a metaphysical as well as physical meaning to her.

It began quite accidentally. She started to run to keep an overweight friend company. The daily 20 to 25 minutes of running became more and more rewarding. Then another good friend, who had been attacked while running alone in a park, asked Celia to run with her once a week. She discovered in running with close friends that half an hour wasn't enough time to conduct a satisfying conversation. So they began running for longer periods, some days "running intervals" (alternating hard runs with slower recovery runs) to build up speed, and eventually running in the New York Marathon. Celia says of this activity:

> The space running occupies in my life is very large. It puts me outside, and I love green, open space. When I run alone, which I do about half the time, I'm out of reach of the telephone and anyone else. And there's something about aerobic breathing that inhibits linear thinking. Something odd happens when you run: your thoughts get shaken out of their grooves, and you begin to think in interesting spirals.
>
> The pleasures of running with someone else are quite different. Running should be done at a pace that permits conversation. Moving with someone, you naturally share back and forth. It's almost impossible to have a monologue. The conversation takes on a rhythm as your body does. I've had some of the best exchanges of my life with three close friends—two women and a man—I run with.
>
> Running does all this for me, quite apart from keeping me healthy and mildly euphoric, and it's all bound up with mastery as well. Day after day, you go out and essentially triumph over whatever is holding you back—whether it's the weather or your sore ankle or your irritability. For me it's not competitive at all, except that I'm competing with myself, asking myself if I can overcome my own resistance, my awkwardness, my fatigue.

Running, Celia says, has changed the physical image of herself she had from childhood on. She grew up in a super-secure, midwestern, English-German family whose slight overprotectiveness contributed to her one insecurity—a fear of taking physical risks, stemming from a sense of herself as physically awkward.

Running has been so crucial to Celia because it became not only a source of mastery and *independent* gratification for her but also the vehicle through which—alone and resonating to some hidden inner tuning fork—she grew more and more certain that something was seriously wrong in her 24-year marriage. It was nothing dramatic, nothing she could precisely localize; that was what had made it so hard to see. But she felt her marriage had become a desert landscape—empty, flat, and dry. "I imagined Jim and me sitting wordlessly across the dinner table night after night over the years for the rest of our lives. And I thought, 'How awful to go into old age like that.'"

While Celia was filling her life with interests and people who had no connection with Jim, he in turn was pulling farther and farther away from her and the family. A free-lance science writer, he spent more and more time in his study, working. His hobby, Indian rock art, became obsessive. This esoteric pursuit required some travel, but it also forced him to spend huge amounts of time in his darkroom or in the studio, fretting over the lightly etched traces he had discovered. His sedentary absorption with the cool rock as Celia turned outward to space and movement seemed emblematic of the growing gulf between them.

Celia also had to acknowledge to herself that she and Jim were just not good for each other, that her competence threatened and depressed him. She had taken the initiative in most family decisions, including planning their family vacations. By 1979 their children were advanced teenagers—Tom was 18 and Laura was 16. At this point, Celia didn't want a family vacation or one with Jim alone. She proposed that this year she and Jim should each take a separate vacation, pursuing separate dreams.

Her own dream was to trek in the Andes. She signed up for a three-week trek with a group and two weeks' travel alone in Peru and Brazil. It was a dream, and it was a risk. Could she handle the physical demands? Would all the others in the group be super-athletes? Would she be able to keep up on the longer, more arduous stretches? Would they be leaping over boulders in mountain streams and walking across scree at dizzying heights that would bring on her acrophobia? Despite all these fears, Celia was very excited. From extensive reading, she knew a good deal about the terrain, the landscape, and the people.

Setting out on the trip not only meant accepting a physical and psychological challenge, it became the first conscious step in confronting her stagnant marriage:

> It was a watershed. Tom had graduated from high school. Laura was a junior. It certainly didn't mean my mothering was over. But my being away five weeks was a way of saying, "You really can handle yourselves without my regular presence." I was also telling Jim, "Now *you* can be the main parent for awhile." I was giving the rest of them the responsibility I had always taken on.

Although Celia worried a fair amount before leaving, from the moment she stepped on the plane, she was euphoric:

> It was a totally magical experience moving through the most beautiful part of the world I could imagine and being on my own after many years of marriage. I slept only a few hours a night, I seemed to have unlimited energy, and I absolutely never crashed. I don't know how much was the altitude, how much the scenery, how much the endless tea we kept drinking. But I was stimulated by everything, and I discovered to my surprise that I was as adept as anyone in the group. Then—to complete the experience—there was a man.

The man—Elliott—was an executive from California who was some eight years older than Celia. He was on the trek without his wife of 35 years. Celia and Elliott fell in love "in a way I had never known before. Imagine meeting the love of your life on a mountain peak in Peru at age 48!" They were bemused yet frightened about their feeling for each other. After the literal descent from the heights, they decided to treat their relationship as a perfect gift box that was to be kept closed, to be reopened only after they had each settled back into their ordinary lives. They agreed not to call each other, not to write for a while, just to assimilate what happened on the mountains.

Meeting Elliott, says Celia, had "everything and nothing" to do with her eventual decision to leave her marriage. She probably would have left eventually anyhow; falling in love with Elliott speeded up the process because it taught her that she could experience real emotional intimacy and that someone could feel that for her. But she left the Andes still determined to make a last-ditch effort to salvage her marriage. During the next six months, Celia tried talking to Jim, spending more time at home, seeing if she and Jim could learn again to treat each other as essential. Jim was kind and available on request, but he didn't respond emotionally or physically. She began to understand that he was and had been chronically depressed.

The six months following her trip were intensely demanding for Celia. She was madly in love and was nevertheless trying to be understanding and giving to Jim. When she and Elliott could no longer stand "keeping the box closed," they made the necessary complicated long-distance travel arrangements to see each other. Celia, a straight arrow, was troubled about deceiving Jim; she applauded Elliott's keen sense of obligation to his wife, who had been a devoted and generous partner for 35 years. As Celia describes it: "I had to be clear about two things: that if I left Jim, it would be to live alone. And that my relationship with Elliott might not last or might consist only of brief encounters. I had to be prepared to live on the edge—committing my feelings to him but knowing it could all end abruptly."

Running and musing, Celia felt the inexorability of her choice: Her marriage was over, she could not go on living that way, she didn't see Jim changing, and she had no more energy to put into their foundering relationship.

At the end of the six months, Celia told Jim that they could not continue their marriage, that she had fallen in love with someone else, and that she had been unfaithful. That was one of the hardest things to tell him. Jim never tried to persuade her to reconsider. On learning about Elliott, he seemed almost relieved, as though separating might give him a new lease on life and pull him out of his stuck place. As Celia observes:

> I think we both came to see that, in some curious way, I'm not good for him. He takes a back seat because of my drive and competence, and then he feels resentful. I was forced to recognize that I defeat his spirit in a way I don't fully understand and that our divorcing might give him the chance to be a happier person.

Once they had agreed, Celia's life entered a new phase—disengaging from being Jim's wife, "like untying a tangled ball of yarn, a knot at a time." The biggest knot was the knot of connection to Jim himself, the giving up of hopes that he could provide what she needed and the acceptance that it was his incapacity—rather than malice or anger—that kept him from providing them.

Another knot was their house. Celia felt that, since she was the instigator, it was only fair that Jim should have the choice about whether to leave or stay. They decided to sell the house to a friend, who would move in after a year; Jim would stay through the summer and then get his own place. Celia would then stay on till the house was sold.

The next knot—the hardest of all—was the children:

> We told them at the dinner table—after the meal—my mother always said to hold off bad news till after you've eaten. I said we had something painful to tell them, that they would probably take it very hard, but that their dad and I had grown farther and farther apart and our lives together weren't what we wanted. That we

thought they were now old enough to handle it. Jim added that this had nothing to do with our feelings for them, and that we were both committed to being there for them whenever they needed it. Tom had tears in his eyes; Laura wailed out words I will never forget, "But we thought the two of you were *immortal*."

The children took it very hard, and for several months the whole family went to a therapist who works with divorcing families. Both Tom and Laura spoke of their shattered sense of optimism. They felt that the separation had "cast them out of childhood," in Tom's words, and made them vulnerable in a way they never had been before. The family continued to live together for the next six months—until the fall, when Laura went away to college. This period may have lasted too long, but it offered them the chance to disengage more gradually and to highlight the things they still had together as a family.

The final knot was telling other people, foremost among whom was Celia's 74-year-old mother. Celia, the "perfect" middle child in a family where her less-achieving siblings had had rocky but intact marriages, had to go to Kansas to tell her mother something none of her children had ever said to her: "I'm getting a divorce." She felt awash in fear:

> . . . a child's kind of fear. I felt very much like a little girl again, wanting so much not to disappoint Mother and knowing that I would.
> Yet her response was not at all what I feared—not outrage or judgment, but just a very great sadness. She was tearful, she had trouble sleeping. And then I caught on: She wasn't feeling critical, she was feeling vulnerable. In fact, *she* was feeling like a child who had lost something terribly important.
> When I realized this, I was able to reassure her that everyone in the family loved her just as much as ever—including Jim—and that she really hadn't lost anyone. I suppose this is the true beginning of advanced middle age: becoming the parent to one's own parents.

Tense as the next few months were, the house served as an anchor. Most trying was the weekend when Jim moved into the condominium he had bought in Manhattan. Celia had been away for the weekend and returned to find the house looking abandoned. Not only were half the possessions gone, according to their agreement, but all the remaining stuff was heaped together, with piles of debris in the middle of the floor.

> I felt like crying, but I couldn't cry then. There were too many things to do. I told myself, "Celia, this is no time to sit down and cry. This has to look like the kids' home when they get back." I think two things saved me from being wildly depressed during all of this, in addition to the running. One was that I was the active agent in most of it. The other, that there was an awful lot to juggle—mostly people I cared about, and then all the financial details to arrange. And, of course, I had the support of a few very dear and old friends.

The closest Celia came to collapsing was shortly after the weekend Jim left. Tom was packing to depart for his second year at college, and Laura had left for her first year. Elliott phoned from the West Coast and told her he had had a major career setback and felt totally shaken and defeated. He said they should stop calling or writing till he got himself together. Then one of Celia's patients, who was the child of a close friend, suffered a serious relapse.

All this happened on a Wednesday, the day Celia runs intervals. "I started running, fighting back tears," Celia recalls. "I ran about a quarter of the distance and then stopped dead, as though I had been sandbagged in the stomach. It really was like smashing up against a buttress. I just stopped and cried for an hour, till I was literally cried out."

Things have improved since then. Elliott has regrouped, and he and Celia still write regularly and see each other every three or four months. Celia has had her first taste of solitude in her large house. She has found it "interesting, sometimes lonely," and she looks forward to living in a smaller space of her own. Jim and she continue to be friendly—most of the time—and they have even talked about having a Christmas dinner together for the family.

What does Celia feel in evaluating this large and difficult risk?

I feel many different things. I guess the first is a more complete perception of myself as a defined person. I've had to make all kinds of decisions alone in the last two years, after decades of basically joint decision making. And I learned how much I hate dishonesty. I couldn't stand being dishonest with Jim. But just as leaving my marriage was what I had to do, I feel that staying in his marriage is what Elliott needs to do.

I feel great sorrow at seeing how hard it's been for Tom and Laura. It has left deep wounds that are still a long way from being healed, though they *are* healing.

And I've learned that I'm more of a loner than I'd thought I was. It's no accident that I found the love of my life more than 4000 miles away, and that he lives 3000 miles from here and is committed.

I'm very sociable, but I look forward to being alone, even to exploring the loneliness. And I'm glad to see that this separation has been good for Jim, who seems to have got his life unstuck. Perhaps we could have staved off the divorce if we'd sought help years ago, but I really feel we did our job together, and it was over.

Perhaps because of the "staid, boring, secure, bedrock" family she grew up in, Celia has had both the need and the confidence to take some plunges. Unlike Jim, whose childhood was more troubled, Celia has the strong sense that she will prevail. On the eve of turning 50, she can say of herself: "I am somewhere near the height of my powers. I feel good about my work. I'm physically strong. I've created a life that I can affirm—with people when they're available, and by myself when they're not."

WHAT WE CAN LEARN FROM CELIA

Celia's risk, like others we have looked at, grew out of emotional pain, increasing hopelessness, and feelings of disuse. It may happen that such pain is not always experienced at its true source, just as someone having a heart attack may experience referred pain in the left arm. Celia found it easier to conclude that her work was the problem than that her marriage was. All this suggests that *for most of us, major life change is not made easily.* It usually takes some external deadline, as with Jenny and Bob, or, as we'll see in the next chapter, some outrage (Jules) or burnout (Gary) or outside pressure (Yvonne) to get us moving. We don't divert the course of our lives lightly or easily—at least, not if we're prudent.

I have observed in my work as a clinician that many people operate from a central metaphor—a concern that captures their life trajectory symbolically. For Celia, the central motif has been *movement*. Running has become important not only in itself but as a physical counterpart of her psychological situation: the desire to move rather than stay put, to exercise her capacities rather than watch them atrophy. Unlike Jim, who *was* atrophying, Celia has a horror of death-in-life. She tends to fight against depression through action—not impulsive, external action, but a disciplined movement both outward and inward. Intense internal work on herself is as important to Celia as physical activity is.

Activity and *agency* are key words, and Celia's sense of being "the active agent in most of it," you will remember, helped to make the rough times easier. Her need for mastery and her willingness to take responsibility for her actions are crucial.

Crucial, too, is her involvement with and caring for others. She has been concerned to strike a balance between meeting her own needs and making life's rigors less painful for those around her. She and Jim have been able to maintain a friendship because they demonstrably did care about each other's well-being. Just as Celia gave to others, she was also able to receive personal and professional support from others.

Celia's divorce process is unusual in extending so long. Some people could not tolerate that much delay. But neither Celia nor Jim is impulsive, and both wanted to give each other and their family time to undo the knots gradually, to ease the transition so that the parting, when it finally came, was less a rupture than a dissolution.

Chapter 5
Models for Risk Taking:
Career-Related Risks

We turn now from risks in which relationships are the primary focus to risks in which career choices are paramount. The three career changers we will consider in this chapter represent three variants of balanced risking: one that is somewhat impulsive (Jules), one that is somewhat constrained (Gary), and one that combines both caution and decisive movement (Yvonne). In reading about these three risk takers, you might take note of which approach is most like yours and hence would work best as a model for you.

CASE HISTORIES

Jules: From New York to California, From Advertising to Psychology

"I discovered I really had a choice!"

Jules illustrates through his geographical move and career change how a basically intuitive person goes about risk taking. His course seems to zigzag, yet there is an internal logic that sets its overall direction. Jules also shows us the importance of *fantasy* in risk taking: how it can be a useful guide to the next step and how it is misleading. Jules is like Carolyn (our Style C example in Chapter 3) in some ways, but very different in others, and those differences are significant. We will also notice in Jules's case what happens when people do not take possible losses into account before risking. Jules's story illustrates the complicated disruptions introduced by a geographical move. It also shows how a move made in desperation can be converted into a satisfying life decision.

* * *

I interviewed Jules Mandel, an attractive, dark-haired, mustached clinical psychologist, on the eve of his fortieth birthday. Sitting in the living room of his Bel Air home, with a sweeping view of the canyon, Jules described for me the cycle of change in his life.

After getting his B.A. from Columbia University in archeology and art history in 1962, Jules had gone into his father's printing business, a comfortable but basically small-time operation, which he helped revamp into a much larger scale enterprise doing high-quality work. All this gave Jules a good deal of satisfaction, but working with his father became too abrasive because of their differences in style and attitude. "My father was ruled by a cautious Depression-era mentality," Jules says. "I was more optimistic, more risk-prone. I wanted to seize the possibilities to expand even more." He finally left and started his own advertising agency.

Things went well. It was 1968 and, as head of his own small agency at 28, he was making between thirty and forty thousand dollars a year. He had bought a Manhattan brownstone, and he was very much part of the New York art/music/ballet scene. He went to all the openings, he had a large circle of friends, and he summered in the Hamptons. But then success reared its Medusa head: Jules landed a major national account, and suddenly he felt overwhelmed—too young and green to play this huge fish. So he went to an established advertising agency for help. They were delighted to have him come and bring his big fish with him. While he was there he met "one of the most brilliant and creative—and controlling—people I've ever known, the agency's creative director." This man (we'll call him Gerson) was as optimistic as Jules and far more experienced. They agreed to form their own firm. But things began to go badly. Gerson's criticality and compulsive need for control had been somewhat diffused in the large agency. Now, with just the two of them, Gerson's pathology was turned on Jules:

> It was constant, badgering accusations. He accused me continually of taking the client's position rather than the agency's, of being disloyal. Any time I questioned him at all, he accused me of being subversive. He had to redo every piece of work I did, and to try to humiliate me in the process.

Their relationship became overwhelmingly adversarial, and the break came without any premeditation. One day Gerson came in, loomed over Jules's desk, and began tearing apart something Jules had written. Jules got up and screamed at him.

> I don't remember what I screamed. I just screamed. And I'm someone who almost never raises my voice. It was like a mini-psychotic episode. I remember walking down the hall in an altered state of consciousness. I remember waiting for the elevator, and then I remember being out on the street about three blocks from my office. I was so blind with rage, those three blocks are a total blank. When I came to, I knew I could never work with Gerson again. Whatever he was doing, I couldn't deal with it.

So that day—or the next, he's not quite sure—he simply told Gerson he was leaving, asked him to draw up the papers dissolving the partnership, checked with his lawyer, and never went back.

Jules left with no plans, not even any ideas. He only knew what he *couldn't* do. He couldn't take his clients with him. He couldn't face the prospect of starting another agency. He didn't want to work in someone else's agency. He had serious questions, in fact, about the whole advertising world.

Several months earlier, Jules had rented a summer house in Amagansett, so he spent the summer there, lying on the beach alone and thinking or, more accurately, "obsessing and worrying" about what would become of him and what he would do. Realistically, he knew he had enough money to tide him over for a while, but his anxiety made him feel poor—shades of his father!

His father's attitudes also dominated the choices Jules was able to give himself at that point. Basically, he felt that he had only two legitimate alternatives: go to work or go to school. The idea of taking a long period off, for pleasure or for healing, didn't occur to him.

What were his work options—his father's business? That had been foreclosed. Advertising again? "I didn't like that world, and most of all I didn't like what I became in that world." Because Jules is naturally a high-spirited extrovert, he had found himself playing that role to the hilt when he worked in agencies, pressuring himself to be "on" all the time. "After the disaster with Gerson, I felt I desperately needed to be quiet for a change, to let things happen rather than forcing them."

If work was not the direction he was seeking, what about school? He decided out of the need for self-help more than because of any career goal to take some introductory psychology courses in the general extension division of his alma mater, Columbia. Because Jules has always learned better from people than from solitary reading, being a student seemed very attractive. He had no sense that he was making a career decision; it was simply a way to keep afloat, to do something acceptable (the only alternative to working) and use it as a way to help himself understand how he'd reached that dead end. The implicit question he was raising for himself was whether people who knew about human psychology knew something that would help him figure out what to do next.

Fortunately, in this vague quest, he happened on a bunch of lively young instructors in Columbia's general extension division. Jules became particularly close to a woman developmental psychologist and began to spin out the fantasy that if he could get a job like hers, he would be dealing with highly motivated students and living a secure life without having to put himself on the line incessantly, as he had in advertising.

This fantasy sustained him while he pursued his year of exploration. The young woman instructor helped hook him into developmental psychology through readings and lectures on Freud, Piaget, and empirical research psychologists. His studies engaged him intellectually as well as personally, and he branched out into more rigorous aspects of psychology, including learning and experimental psychology. "I finally had some constructs," he says, "that I could use to make sense of other people and myself."

Working with his therapist, he came to see that his liking for people and for teaching could readily combine in an academic career. Having been to the West Coast several years earlier, Jules had fallen in love with Los Angeles, and he decided he wanted to go to UCLA for graduate training.

He applied, and he was accepted. With the money he had made from selling his New York brownstone and his shares in the family business, he took a leisurely cross-country trip with a woman friend who also planned to study at UCLA. "We were like Hansel and Gretel setting out, full of hope and optimism." So sanguine was he that he remembers thinking, in a burst of grandiosity as the New York skyline receded, "How will New York manage without me? Doesn't it know what it's losing?"

The other side of the coin—what *he* was losing in leaving New York— didn't become visible for a while. At first, Jules was busy furnishing the Bel Air house he had bought as soon as he arrived in Los Angeles. Visitors came often that year, and Jules was feeling buoyant. He had chosen to redefine himself in a beautiful, stimulating place with many unknown possibilities. He grew his hair long, he grew a beard, and he experimented with LSD; he became flushed with the idea that this time his success would be his own, not based on his father's enterprise or his involvement with a partner. What he missed, fleetingly, were "the people—and the pastrami!"

Jules was very busy at school, and he did well, but he found that developmental psychology wasn't quite what he had been looking for. He also came to see that the tranquility and peace of academia were really the products of his fantasy. Watching his professors at work and behind the scenes, he realized that an academic career might not necessarily give him more autonomy or more freedom from backbiting than he had known in advertising.

What Jules felt in this initial year in Los Angeles was mostly relief and excitement, with a slightly uneasy undercurrent about his career choice and the people he had left behind. About a year after he entered graduate school, a close relationship broke up, and a New York friend died. These losses released the memories of *all* the unmourned connections he had broken when he left New York so blithely. As waves of loss and disaffection engulfed him, he sought comfort—and possibly illumination—in LSD:

> I took a real strong hit of acid. I had never had a trip like this before. I had the experience of exploding into a million diamonds in the room and of coming together completely different. It was exhilarating and frightening. I was alone, and at some point I got to a phone and began talking to a friend. The conversation lasted four hours, and what I was saying in all sorts of different ways was, "I don't want to go to school."
>
> At that point I walked out my front door and said to my next-door neighbor, who was watering his lawn, "Don, I don't have to go to school." And he said to me, "Jules, who ever said you *did*?" That really stopped me. That may have been the most important moment of my life: *I discovered I really had a choice*! It took the acid and Don's remark to blast me out of the obligatory principle of doing the right thing, doing the one thing that's acceptable.
>
> So instead of tilting blindly forward, I withdrew. I took the year off and did nothing, just hung out and met people. I really established myself in the area, putting down roots for the first time. That gave me the sense that I wasn't just a transient or just a student but that I could stay in this city and build a life here.
>
> During that period I began to stop thinking of myself as wrong and broken. I

realized I had been coping pretty well with everything. For the first time in my life, I felt real.

My "dropping out" for a year makes me think of an anecdote Sidney Morgenbesser, my old Columbia philosophy professor told about George Santayana, who one May day dismissed one of his Harvard classes early, saying, "Sorry, gentlemen, I have a date with spring." Taking a year off to find where I wanted to go was like my saying, "Sorry, gentlemen, I have a date with life."

After this year of belated moratorium, comparable to the year off many young people now take between high school and college or at some other time in their late adolescence, Jules at 32 had become sure of what he wanted to do: he wanted to become a clinical psychologist, to have his own autonomous practice, to work directly and closely with people, and occasionally to teach.

Once he knew what he wanted, the rest was easy. He was recommended to a select seminar taught by a nationally renowned psychologist who was an outstanding researcher and expert in psychological assessment. This older woman became first Jules's mentor and then his closest friend. "I learned most of what I know about psychotherapy from her—either directly or by her example. I learned how to work with people currently and in the future, rather than eternally plumbing the old cesspool. My first clients were those she referred to me. Through her, my network of social support got built up and has continued to sustain me." Although he feels that "subliminally it was *all* risky," the only time Jules experienced acute danger was after he quit the partnership, because he knew he was leaving something but didn't have the vaguest notion of where he was going. "I only knew that everything I had done over the previous ten years I could not do any more."

As a result, the summer in Amagansett was the most upsetting time of his life. In retrospect, Jules says that if he had it to do over now, he would perhaps give himself the option that he could not have given himself then, the option that came as a demand several years later when he indeed did drop out. But really, Jules says, he isn't given to regrets, because everything he did seems to have had a relation to what he has become:

> The need to do something so I wouldn't go crazy drove me back to school. I know now that I could have quit the partnership with the paranoid loon sooner and saved myself grief. But experiencing that grief has helped me in my work with clients in similar no-win situations to move in more directly by labeling the dead ends and helping them cut their losses.

Jules believes that life is a series of constant problems to be solved; one's style imposes the individual logic or rhythm on this process. Thus, *there are almost no decisions that are in themselves absolutely right or wrong. It's what we do with their fallout that matters.*

WHAT WE CAN LEARN FROM JULES

Jules's risk-taking style is highly intuitive. He often proceeds on hunch without attempting to spread out all the alternatives open to him. His motto seems to be: "How do I know what I want till I see what I do?" To such a person, the way is often found in *illuminations*. Two major decisions (to quit the partnership and to drop out of school) both came in the altered states of consciousness produced in one case by rage and in another by LSD. For creative, intuitive people who are not given to the work-a-day process of meticulously laying out and scanning alternatives, "Truth comes in blows," as Saul Bellow has written.

Jules's decision making has an improvisatory look, as though it were a piecemeal attempt to deal with the consequences of each move as they occur. But the process is not as disconnected or erratic as it sounds, because, underlying his somewhat impulsive surface, Jules has a strong sense of self. He also has confidence not only that he will endure but that he will nourish himself from what happens. Instead of planning, he often appears to be set moving by *fantasy:* the fantasy of academia, the fantasy of California. These fantasies serve to get him going; later they must be corrected because of their illusionary quality.

This intuitive, feeling-oriented strategy can only work with people who have (1) a high degree of imagination and flexibility; (2) a tolerance for ambiguity; and (3) probably most important, the certitude that the consequences, whatever they are, will be both informative and manageable.

Jules lives with a constant sense of becoming, of defining and redefining himself in the course of what he does. This perception of life-in-progress is not shared by everyone. Some people—as we shall see from the examples that follow—need much greater structure and certainty in making major choices.

Another issue we can notice in Jules's life change is the importance of other people—particularly women—as teachers, stimulators, and bridges. Since Jules had no one else to consider directly in making his major vocational and geographical change, his decision, he notes, was easier than it would have been for someone who had to take into account its effect on others. But that does not mean that other people were not highly important in reducing the risks. Jules managed in his personal and professional life to derive support and guidance when he needed them—from the young instructor in developmental psychology, from the "Gretel" with whom he made the cross-country trip, from the woman who became his mentor and friend. Indeed, Jules has found *people* as providers of support and information more useful than intensive, isolated reading, self-scrutiny, or list making.

Despite the intuitive or improvisatory appearance of his choices, Jules does tend to *build bridges* to the new territory. Although he came 3,000 miles across the country, he came with a close friend. His very *un*impulsive amassing of equity in his New York brownstone and in his father's business provided the financial underpinning to support him through graduate school in a style that did not require belt cinching.

Jules's style could be described as a modified version of "fly now, pay later." Instead of mourning in anticipation, he tends to register his losses after the fact. Thus, his pain at leaving New York didn't really hit him until some years afterward. In fact, his first reaction was a kind of defensive reversal: "New York ought to miss me!" This style may help him to act decisively, whereas reckoning of the losses beforehand actually might have inhibited his leaving.

What makes Jules's action-oriented style not truly impulsive, like Carolyn's (our Style C exemplar), is his *sense of consequence*. Although he does not always deliberately anticipate them, he is fully aware that his actions will have consequences—some of them unpleasant and difficult—and he is prepared to pay the price in an ungrudging willingness to convert "mistakes" into lessons. As he puts it: "When you've got lemons, you make lemonade." So he's not surprised if things turn out badly; he simply registers that outcome as a problem to be solved, and then he takes the next step.

Gary: From Probation Officer To Restaurateur

"Quitting felt so good the third time."

Gary's story raises a number of issues, among them: the consequences of choosing a career by chance, quitting versus exploring options while on the job, and how it feels to make a "real choice" in a career. It also raises the question of whether taking a major risk makes it more likely that you will take another. Stylistically, Gary is on the cautious end of balance. It took him a long time, and much agonizing to make a large career change.

* * *

Gary Weber, 38, sits over a glass of white wine in the courtyard of his small, chic Mill Valley restaurant—we'll call it Spencer's—at 4:30 in the afternoon, between the lunch and dinner crunch. He talks with me of the road that has led him here, while a busboy interrupts with questions, a waiter asks for a key to the storeroom, and two board members of the local repertory theater drop by to thank him for contributing the house specialty—pine-nut tarts—for their gala opening.

Amid it all, Gary appears unflustered. If it's possible to be intense in a low-keyed way, Gary is. He cares a lot about what he is telling me, but his blue eyes look rather sleepy. If he's anxious, as he says he often is, it doesn't show in his almost catlike calm. With his brown hair—slightly graying, thin on top and full at the sides—and his yellow oxford-cloth shirt and jeans, he looks more like an executive taking his ease on the weekend than the harried proprietor of a fledgling restaurant still trying to shake out its wings and fly.

Gary is interested in change, and he warms to the topic as he talks, because he sees it all around him and feels that his own pattern is typical:

> I see more and more people who ten or fifteen years ago would have been expecting a long, steady path to the top of their chosen fields. Now they're not taking that route. Somewhere in the middle they begin to rethink what they want, and it's not just to change jobs within a field but to change fields completely.

Gary himself has tried both. For the first ten years of his professional life, he tried changing jobs within a field. After that, he changed his line of work drastically. This is the story of that process.

When he graduated in 1964 from San Francisco State University, with a B.A. in social science and a sprinkling of accounting courses, Gary expected to teach economics and history in high school. But he learned from a friend that the county probation office was looking for college graduates with social science backgrounds as group counselors. Gary liked young people, he had practice-taught in inner-city schools, and he strongly wanted to do work that was socially useful. The added bonus was that probation work would give him a draft deferment.

So he signed on as a group counselor in Boys' Ranch—a hundred acres of open, flat land, covered with tomato plants and almond trees, near Stockton, California. In this institution for delinquent boys ages 14 to 17, Gary was assigned as counselor to eight to ten boys on the daytime shift, working with each boy to identify his problems, his strengths, his school deficiencies, his drug history, and so on. Gary got on-the-job training through daily community meetings and by observing how experienced probation officers dealt with the kids. The work was scary at first, requiring that Gary do a lot of commonsense, seat-of-the-pants improvising, but on the whole it was gratifying.

Gary liked the work, and he grew in it: "I had had a fairly safe and unreflective life till then as an only child who'd been in school for 17 years. But working in probation you have to do a tremendous amount of soul searching or you can't survive. I was forced to clarify who I was, what I valued. You can't train someone else in values without looking seriously at your own."

In the course of this soul searching, Gary found that he wanted more status, more variety, and—since he had just gotten married—more money. After two years at Boys' Ranch, he passed the test for probation officer and got a high-paying, more demanding job. In February 1967, he started a harrowing assignment as probation officer in the black ghetto of North Richmond, California:

> On my second day—I'll never forget it—a white sheriff's officer had shot a black kid during a misdemeanor. The black community was justifiably outraged, and the Black Panthers, then a fairly new organization, showed up en masse. The county building was right across from the jail. I had to go into the county building past this file of Black Panthers—Eldridge Cleaver, Bobby Seale, Huey Newton, and the others—all standing there, rifles up, in full gear, with berets and bandoliers. They looked fierce. Not the weaponry, but the fury and hatred you could almost touch. I was 24 and terrified. But I thought, "If I can handle the institution, I can handle this." You could feel that ominous presence even when you went up 11 floors in the county building. But no violence occurred.

During the next two years, Gary worked tirelessly, spending less time at home with his wife, Linda, than he would have liked. He had as many as 110 to 120 youngsters in his caseload at a time. Moreover, since his territory was the outskirts of the county, there was almost no public transportation. As a result, he spent hours and hours driving from school to school and from courthouse to courthouse. He also spent hours and hours writing the lengthy investigative reports required by the courts after a petition had been filed. In his sleep at night he felt he was still driving, still writing field notes. "And," he says with a snort, "you were supposed to change the boys' behavior by seeing them once a month."

Gary took a year of this and then transferred to a different district, which had developed a more experimental and humane program. For the next two and a half years, he saw only ten boys at a time, working with them intensively every day and feeling that he was making a real impact. He also tutored them and worked with the parents as well. He felt he was really connecting with each of his ten charges and making a difference.

But trouble with a reactionary judge and the firing of Gary's supervisor filled him with the dread that, no matter how effective he was as an individual, he couldn't buck the ossified probation system. As usual, when Gary felt disgruntled, he thought not about leaving but about transferring. His next job within the probation field—investigating cases of child neglect and child abuse—was "the worst year I've ever spent," leaving him sickened, his capacity for compassion drained.

By August 1974, Gary had served close to ten years in the California probation system. Although he had always had the same title—probation officer—his work had taken him into ranches and ghettos, into homes and courts, into schools and county offices. He felt he had grown "at least 20 years" during those ten, but much of that growth was agonizing, and much of what he had seen infuriated him:

> In court I often saw incompetent attorneys abusing people, and the abuse seemed proportionate to the lack of income. I had seen those who didn't rock the boat get promoted. If you were at all your own person, if you questioned anyone in authority, you might as well kiss off.
>
> I was pretty good at my job. I could do my work in four hours a day. But there was no incentive to be creative. I took a ceramics course. Then I studied real estate and began selling real estate in my slack time—feeling justified yet guilty. Worst of all, I was beginning to burn out on the kids, and that scared me.

On August 16, 1974—Gary remembers the exact date—he and Linda were sitting on their patio and talking. She had been working as a teacher-counselor in a public school and was earning a reasonably good salary. They were looking at a plate Gary had made in a ceramics workshop:

> My wife said, "Gary, you're a creative person, a talented person. But this job is wiping you out. You're miserable, you have headaches. Please quit."
>
> Her giving me the psychological permission to do what I'd been wanting to do was like opening a dam. I took her hand, and I just cried. I was so happy, so relieved. I didn't have any idea what I wanted to do. I just knew I had interests and talents, and intelligence, and energy if I could recapture it—and I'd make it.
>
> Quitting this time wasn't going toward something. It was going away. I knew if I stayed I would become just like the rest of them: a defeated person sweating out ten more years till retirement.

Gary also realized that he had never made an active decision to become a probation officer. Chance and circumstances had pushed him into it. He wanted for once in his life to choose work that was really his.

So he quit and spent the next year and a half exploring options and recuperating while his wife taught school. He made and sold his pottery. He took some courses. He kept up with his real estate, but the firm was doing badly. This was a troubled time, a time in which he experienced great mood swings. He felt overwhelmingly relieved not to be working in probation, but he was still unsure about what his real skills and interests were. He was beginning to have a clearer idea of what he *didn't* want. He felt he could make only a marginal living from being a potter, and he didn't want that. He also knew that the life of a craftsman was too solitary for someone who liked people as much as he did. It was the people part of real estate he liked, and he would spend time doing favors for his clients that went far beyond the bounds of the job.

In a dim way, he knew he wanted to do something for and with people and to make a decent living, but he didn't know how to put those puzzle pieces together. At 34, he still had no idea what he wanted to be "when he grew up." But being without a second income was putting too much strain on Gary and Linda, especially now that they had a child. The outcome of that difficult time was that he decided to go back to probation "for just a year or so" and to spend that time really educating himself about what he wanted to do. He had decided that it might be easier to search within a secure context than to make the search the sole focus of his life.

Gary spent the following year and a half working and exploring. He researched all sorts of possibilities: city planning and architecture, accounting, and landscape gardening. He met with Richard Bolles, author of the guide to career planning, *What Color Is Your Parachute?*. He used computer matching systems. He talked to friends. Since he could do his job effectively in four hours a day, the rest of the time he worked on his career. Pieces began fitting together in a way that was somewhat surprising to him.

> I realized that I loved to cook. I had worked in food services in college and had cooked a lot for my parents as a kid, because my mother was working. I liked being around people. I wanted to work for myself. I have a certain skepticism—sometimes downright hostility—toward authority. I wanted to sink or swim on my own merits. I wanted to run something in a creative, upbeat atmosphere. As I put all this together, I began for the first time to consider going into the restaurant business.

Gary didn't want to be a chef; about four hours a day in the kitchen is his maximum. He wanted public contact, and for that part of restaurant work he needed management and business skills. He was too impatient and too old, he felt, to go back to school. In talking to the manager of a fast-food restaurant where he'd eaten breakfast for the past two and a half years, he discovered that the parent chain had a first-rate training program. One day he told the manager, "Bud, I'd like to learn the restaurant business," and Bud agreed to take him on. After thinking about it for two days, Gary walked into the probation department and said he was quitting. His co-workers all told him in different ways that he was crazy, but he could see the envy in their eyes.

Quitting was much easier this time, because Gary knew he wasn't just running away from something into the nebulous night. He was moving toward something specific for the first time. True, his salary would plunge to less than half of what he'd been earning as a probation officer, but he and Linda were prepared to scrimp for a while.

For the next 19 months, Gary worked in the restaurant, quickly scaling the ladder from the second assistant manager on the night shift (driving home dog-tired at 3 a.m.) to first assistant manager on the day shift, and finally to manager of one of the largest-grossing restaurants in the 600-unit chain. "When I started as manager I was more scared than at Boys' Ranch," he recalls. "My present job is *retirement* in comparison. We had 35 employees working around the clock. The pressure was unbelievable. Although the days sped by, every one was like a week in terms of what I was learning about equipment, personnel, ordering, customer relations, record keeping, quality control... you name it."

Shortly after Gary started as manager, Sarah Spencer, a young woman who was running an inn in Mendocino, heard about him through friends. She was by instinct and training an inventive cook, but she had little feel for business. She came to Gary for advice on cost-accounting for her inn. The two became good friends, and they began to spin a joint fantasy of opening a place together that would combine the special talents of each. By this time, Gary had learned that he loved the restaurant business, that his counseling skills could be used in dealing with employee problems and in making customers feel good, that as a restaurateur you got immediate feedback from your decisions, and that even the accounting part was satisfying. So Gary and Sarah decided to open a restaurant in Mill Valley, California.

This time quitting was very easy. As Gary describes it: "Quitting felt so good the third time. Having quit twice before, I finally managed to overcome my fears. I had retrained myself. I was marketable. I knew I could get a job anywhere in the world now. I was self-confident for the first time. I knew what I wanted to do, and I knew I could do it."

Gary quit without having found a site, but he and Sarah were looking hard. By Christmas, two months later, they had found a site that instantly appealed to them: a small office building with a redwood exterior and an enclosed court. Gary became exceedingly anxious during the money-raising phase. The prime rate had gone up to 18 to 20 percent, and no one would lend them anything at less than 22 percent. It was "pure hustle," he says, which meant taking out second and third deeds of trust on his house, getting loans through friends, capitalizing on his real estate experience.

Good luck favored him in the form of a young designer who wanted to get some commercial experience and offered to design the restaurant's interior at a very low fee. Their idea was to create "a total format for dining"—from the setting to the preparation and presentation of the food. Sarah and Gary wanted a light, airy ambience; they wanted their restaurant to be more sleek and chic, more "urban" than the wood-and-hanging-plant, organic-food atmosphere that characterizes most Mill Valley eating places. They decided on white and black tile floors, Breuer chairs, and tables in the courtyard. They also sought to keep the menu fresh, light, and free from any national label. "You could call it Northern California, with a twist," Gary says. "We're free to draw on French, Italian, and Greek cuisine, but the emphasis is on fresh local ingredients presented with a fillip, like our salad of broiled duck livers, escarole, and hazelnuts."

Spencer's opened in June 1980 with a staff of 23 people, many of them artists and writers seeking to supplement their income in a congenial environment. It reached the break-even point slightly ahead of schedule. In a town noted for sophisticated palates and a great number of restaurants, Spencer's has accumulated a devoted following. Gary spends most of his time (13 hours a day, 6 days a week) outside the kitchen, where he defers to Sarah. Commenting on the chance he took in starting this entirely new career, he says: "This felt so risky—and still does—that I can hardly believe I'm doing it. As you can tell from how hard it was to leave probation work, I am not a risk-taking person. But I do remember hearing my father say again and again as he got older, 'If only I'd a done this,' and 'If only I'd a done that.' I swore I'd never say that."

Although Gary doesn't risk easily, he does have a restless spirit and a need to keep learning. Even now he is thinking ahead to his next move,

> For my next venture, I want to make money—a lot of money. Not because I'm hooked on creature comforts or need to live in high style, but because my goal now is to be able to retire at 50—12 years from now. One way or another, I've worked since I was 12, and I'm looking forward to the day I can throw off the Protestant work ethic I've lived by most of my life. My aim in making it big financially would be to stop working while I still have energy, and to spend the rest of my life building fences, throwing pots, reading, and taking time for my friends and family.

Ideally, Gary would like to retire to a farm, but Linda is strictly a city person. "I love my wife very much," Gary says, unself-consciously, "and I'm prepared to make the same kinds of sacrifices for her that she did for me."

In evaluating his risk, Gary comments that even if Spencer's doesn't make it, this venture will have been worthwhile because it has freed him to take other chances. He now knows that with his own inner resources and with the support of his family, he not only will survive—he will prevail.

WHAT WE CAN LEARN FROM GARY

By his own admission, Gary is not a risk taker. He moves slowly and carefully, and he takes into account the needs and wishes of those who are close to him.

Gary's difficult work history stemmed partly from his entering probation work out of *expediency* rather than *conviction*. Many of us start out in the world of work this way. Gary's was not a catastrophic or inappropriate choice, but it left many of his deepest needs unsatisfied, and he never really claimed the choice as his. Although he had the skills to be a good counselor, he found more and more that he could not use them within the probation system. At first he adopted a conservative strategy: change within the field. Looking at Gary's work history, we could describe him equally well as a restless maverick or as a cautious play-it-safer, depending on what we chose to emphasize. The truth is probably a paradoxical mixture. Gary is a restless man who needs frequent change, but until recently he has been afraid of drastic change. As a result, he tried to meet both these needs by staying in a system and changing positions within it. That strategy of making small, incremental changes worked up to a point, until his feeling of waste and burnout became too acute.

Like Jules, Gary took some time out. Given his temperament, however, that year and a half was not the fruitful period of discovery he had hoped it would be; instead, it was simply a necessary "breather" that enabled him to go back into the fray. Both his temperament and the added demands for security posed by having a family made Gary's sabbatical different from Jules's time out.

Gary discovered that he could explore more actively while he was working than while he was not. For many people, having free time, instead of begetting ideas and impulses, opens up vistas of terrifying emptiness. Gary found it easier to carry on his personal search while he had more structure in his life. Also, unlike Jules, he was really methodical in canvassing alternatives.

When Gary hit upon his "real choice," he felt he had not invented it but *discovered* it, as though it were there all along, waiting to be unearthed. This feeling of "rightness" is like the feeling you get when you try various keys that don't work and finally stumble on the one that clicks the lock open.

This "click" of rightness, of saying yes with your whole being, means that you have managed to bring together aspects of yourself that in the past were represented only piecemeal.

Dealing with people had attracted Gary to probation work and to real estate; the idea of a creative product that was useful and pleasing drew him to pottery. He could combine these talents in the restaurant by creating an environment, a bill of fare, and a staff that would bear his own stamp.

In addition to drawing together disparate parts of himself, the restaurant has helped him develop a neglected side, which neither his probation work nor his pottery had nourished: a flair for entrepreneurship, for running his own show. Gary's history tells us that *when we change fields in midlife, we must find work that is connected in some way with things we have done before*, so that we need not feel we have repudiated our entire past. *But the work must also go beyond our past* to allow a previously unhonored aspect of the self to emerge. These criteria help us experience ourselves both as continuous and as growing, and they hark back to the idea of *change within structure* that I outlined earlier.

As a result of these experiences, Gary is now a more confident risk taker than he ever has been. His experience in "quitting the third time" has convinced him that he will continue to venture and that his life, like his pots, is his to shape—with all due regard and care for the others who share it with him.

Yvonne: A Career Change at 45

"Being fired wasn't a disaster; it was an opportunity."

In Yvonne's methodical risk-taking style great energy is exerted in exploring a large number of possibilities and covering all bases. We will see how the crucial permission Yvonne gave herself in her search enabled her to convert an *imposed* risk to a *chosen* one. Other issues include the relative balance of information seeking and support seeking in Yvonne's career change and the difference in style in her personal as opposed to her professional risks.

* * *

Yvonne Crawford talked to me from behind her office desk in a Cleveland highrise that houses the head office of the retailing chain for which she works. A slim woman of medium height, Yvonne is dressed casually and smartly in a tweed suit. Her short, black hair is sparked with gray; she has high cheekbones, a large, aquiline nose, and blue eyes that glint behind lavender-tinted aviator glasses. Yvonne projects a practical, no-nonsense image, with just a hint of romanticism.

In 1979, she was a woman on the way up, but she had been down for some time. A number of years earlier, a physical illness had forced her to give up a career in merchandising to do less strenuous things, such as volunteering for the League of Women Voters and taking courses for a master's degree in public administration. Her marriage had ended in divorce several years earlier. But she had recouped and worked her way up in a metropolitan transportation agency to become director of public affairs, with an excellent salary, a staff of eight, and hopes for a long and increasingly fruitful career.

What Yvonne could not have anticipated in taking this job was the lack of understanding the technical staff, composed largely of engineers, would have for the work she was doing. When a new executive director was brought in from a state agency not noted for its attempts to inform or involve the public, the tension increased.

After a few months, Yvonne decided to have a talk with this man:

> It was a real scene. I was very forthright with him and surprisingly emotional for me. I've rarely gotten that charged up at work, but I was all choked up with frustration. I told him I felt he was unsympathetic to my role in the agency. He simply refused to level back—really, he just didn't respond. And I left with a blur of tears in my eyes.

On a Monday, two weeks later, the executive director called her into his office and, without warning and without having given her a job review, told her that agency budget reductions made it necessary to cut down on staff by discontinuing both her job and that of the deputy director.

Although he said it was strictly a budgetary issue, Yvonne didn't really believe him and felt in any case that he had handled the situation with a callous disregard for her feelings. Stunned and unstrung, she took some things out of her desk and headed home. Since she had never lost a job before, Yvonne experienced it as a tremendous blow:

> I was in shock. I had to cancel a meeting for later that day. When I did feel something, it was terror. I'd lose my house; I wouldn't be able to pay my bills. I wouldn't be able to feed my cat, who is incredibly dear to me. Never before had I been in the position of not having a job when I wanted one. It was terrifying to realize how much of my life as a woman alone depended on that. I needed the job for the tangible things that had become important to me, but even more, I needed it for my identity. So at first I was scared. I didn't feel angry till a little later.

Actually, the decision to change jobs had been germinating in Yvonne's mind for some time before it was so rudely thrust on her. A year before, she had gone to a professional seminar on making career changes and had completed a series of exercises to identify her transferable skills. She already knew she was tired of citizens "yammering away" at public servants, particularly after the passage of a drastic amendment that severely limited state funding. So it was no accident that on her bedside table at the moment she was laid off was Richard Irish's book, *If Things Don't Improve Soon, I'm Going to Ask You to Fire Me.*

Still, there is a difference between choosing to leave and being asked to leave—the difference between the chosen and the imposed risk. Fortunately, Yvonne is a "doer" whose self-preservative instincts usually see her through.

Her first move was to call a friend, who gave her the name of an extremely talented career counselor (we'll call her Mitzi). Yvonne made an appointment to see Mitzi the next day, a Wednesday. She survived Black Monday and Blue Tuesday, and on Wednesday she presented herself to Mitzi. Still feeling "cast aside," as though she had done something wrong, she nevertheless was determined to keep moving and to explore her network of friends and former associates.

In a tribute to what a gifted counselor can do, Yvonne notes:

Mitzi did a remarkable piece of work. In an hour and a half she completely turned me around. She showed me clearly something I had already half-acknowledged: that I really didn't like that job, that there was therefore no point in fighting to keep it, that being fired wasn't a disaster—it was an opportunity. Being able to see her right away and to make the 180-degree turn gave me the optimism I needed to keep going. In fact, somewhat to my surprise, the six-month period that followed was probably the best time of my life. It was very stimulating. I felt completely in control. I loved setting my own schedule. I took myself as my project, I worked like a dog, and I accomplished a whole lot.

The first thing Yvonne did was to negotiate with the agency for maximum severance pay. She talked to a former boss, who was appalled and very supportive, and she sought out another friend in a public agency, who encouraged her, shared her outrage, and gave her advice about what to ask for. She negotiated an extra month's severance pay and a letter indicating that the job had been discontinued (rather than submitting her resignation, as they had originally requested). All this permitted her to clear her name and become eligible for unemployment compensation if she needed it.

The next step was to sit down and assess her net worth in savings, stock, and real estate, so that she could calculate how long she could survive without a job. Her salary would continue for two months, and she figured she could survive for nine months after that. This meant giving herself permission to draw on resources she had been saving for a rainy day. "It was frightening to do, but I had to admit to myself that this really *was* a rainy day."

Good fortune stepped in to provide a little sunlight when a former colleague called and offered Yvonne a chance to write a chapter of a book on the state's urban strategies program. The $5000 contract put a little more distance between her and the poorhouse and also gave her a peg to hang her identity on while she was rethinking her career. She used some of that $5000 as seed money for "investing," as Yvonne puts it, in her job search: buying a fancy typewriter, paying for an answering service, having calling cards and attractive letterhead designed and printed, getting her revised résumé duplicated.

During the months that followed, Yvonne thought hard about what she wanted and what she didn't want. Despite her interest in government and her graduate training in public administration, Yvonne had been burned by her public affairs experience. "I'd given the public ten years of hard service, and it seemed as though I'd have to be a masochist to continue along that route." Although she pretty well ruled out government jobs, she nevertheless made very sure to maintain all her contacts in the professional organizations for which she had planned conferences and chaired committees.

During the two months Yvonne was still on salary, she intensively and systematically explored her network of friends and professional associates and applied for a total of 49 jobs. Some of these merely required writing a letter. About 15 went to the interview stage, and one of them—a big banking job—required nine interviews during a single day.

Yvonne did a fair amount of research during this period, because several of the jobs were in fields she knew little about. One of these was the executive directorship of a local nurses' association that was empowered to negotiate with hospital administrators. After her initial interview, Yvonne went back to the association board and asked them a series of tough questions she would have to have answered before deciding whether she and the job were a good match: Who really had the power in the organization? What kinds of skills were they looking for? What was the grant of authority for the executive director? These questions were met by a somewhat uncomfortable silence, and it soon became clear to the association representatives that they had to postpone the search until they clarified for themselves what the job truly entailed.

Another job for which she interviewed was the nine-interview position as public information director for a large regional bank system. She lost out on the job. "It went to a man," she says somewhat ruefully, "and I felt bad about that for half a day or so, but I began to realize that the job would have meant more pressure and probably greater visibility than I felt comfortable with right then."

Characteristically, though, Yvonne didn't let slip all the hard work she had done in pursuing the bank job. Taking her cue from a book she has found very helpful (*Jobsearch,* by H. Lee Rust), she didn't simply write a pro forma note ("I'm sorry to hear the job was filled; thank you for your time."). Instead, she drafted a letter to the vice-president for public affairs, with whom she had had several conversations.

> I wrote something like: "I'm really sorry to hear that the job has been filled. I thought I'd be terrific. I also very much appreciate the time you spent talking to me. Because you know so much about banking, I would like to keep in touch with you from time to time as I continue my search. Would that be okay?" He replied very graciously, and I had lunch with him several times after that and got some more leads.

During her time-out period, Yvonne also seriously considered an idea that had intrigued her for several years: going into business for herself. Three possibilities tempted her:

1. Becoming a consultant on public affairs in the private sector or for government. She actually submitted a proposal for this kind of position to a government agency that had put out a request for such a proposal. (Unfortunately, the request for proposal was later withdrawn because of lack of funds.)

2. Buying into a regional magazine directed at women, as a local publisher. Again she researched this operation, looking at local advertising possibilities and resources for financing. She carefully reviewed a sample copy and decided it was too "lightweight" to interest her; but in the course of reviewing the issue she offered the company a critique, containing some suggestions of what she would do differently.

3. Franchising a service for working people. This idea, she says, is so

good that she's reluctant to say more about it, especially since she may decide to go ahead and develop it one day.

After pondering all the self-employment possibilities and taking a couple of workshops on small businesses, she decided that her bottom line was "more stability—that paycheck coming in regularly." In the course of her reading and talking and self-scrutiny, Yvonne came up with a mental balance sheet that had large pluses next to government experience (ten years), retailing experience (eight years as a fashion buyer), and public relations skills. She felt that she should be able to put those skills together in one satisfying package.

By mid-July, two months after the money had stopped coming in, she had narrowed her goal to public affairs work in a retail enterprise. Her ex-husband, with whom she is still friendly, helped with suggestions. Finally, she had a list of three firms. Two of them had no openings or interest in public affairs. The third was the one she really wanted most. It was a retail operation I'll call Goodwin's—a soft-goods chain (clothing, linens, domestics, toys), with 69 branch stores in six states. Goodwin's was remarkable for its policy of giving 5 percent of its pretax income for public interest causes. Working for this firm would combine Yvonne's interest in public, nonprofit enterprises and her earlier experience in retailing. "Because Goodwin's isn't a polluter, because it's not trying to make profits on the backs of its workers, because it has excellent salaries, and because it does have this public interest emphasis, it's an ideal public relations client. You simply have to spread the good word," Yvonne says.

With this idea in mind, Yvonne began a focused, high-gear job campaign. She wrote to the vice-president of personnel and made a series of phone calls to top management. "Eventually," she says, "they decided I was serious. There was no real job, just my persistence." Her first interview, with the vice-president for personnel and the vice-president for sales, lasted four hours—making her two hours late for a dinner date with a man who had been waiting at her house!

The company brass was very positive, but the only opening they had was a relatively junior job, writing press releases. Yvonne kept on, trying to convince them they needed something more ambitious. At her next interview, she brought her own proposal, outlining what a professional public affairs person could do for Goodwin's in a more spacious conception of public information. The result: they offered her the job she had designed, and they matched her previous salary.

Yvonne was tempted to say yes on the spot. Thinking that might look eager and unjudicious, however, she feigned coolness and asked for a day to mull it over. She didn't need that day, because the momentum of her search had led her straight to this job, and she knew she wanted it. She accepted it with the proviso that she be allowed a one-month grace period. For the next two weeks, she put herself on a crash schedule, writing ten pages a day to finish the chapter she had agreed to write for her former colleague. Then she went to Tahiti and Bora Bora for a well-earned two-week vacation, dropping her chapter off en route to the airport in a photo finish.

How has it worked out? "About the way I expected," Yvonne reflects. "Mostly very well, although the job hasn't grown quite as fast as I want to see it grow. I'd like a larger staff and a full-time secretary, but that will come in time." Her fantasy is to become a vice-president for public affairs/community relations. This post doesn't exist, but if Yvonne has her way, it will, because she most enjoys the public affairs part of her job, which draws on her skill in lobbying and working with retail associations and legislators.

Does she have any regrets? "Absolutely none." In fact, she says, it may have been lucky that she was let go rather than quitting, because she might not have done such a thorough job search if she hadn't felt pressed: "A good job search can take an awfully long time. Some counselors figure it takes between one and two years, the length being proportionate to the level at which you're looking. So I was fortunate to get my job in only six months. But, of course, I did work like a demon at it."

Her feelings about herself as a result of this process are overwhelmingly positive. "I think I'm terrific," she grins, "but then I've always had a natural optimism about work; being 45 made me a little anxious, but my age didn't seem to be a barrier."

On the other hand, her personal life still has some big gaps. "It's seven years since my divorce," she says, "and I never would have believed I'd be single after that much time. I have had a number of relationships, but none that has worked out as I'd hoped. I wish I could change my personal life as easily as I changed my work life. I've almost always been considerably less venturesome when it came to relationships than when it came to jobs."

WHAT WE CAN LEARN FROM YVONNE

Yvonne is not a plunger. She has confidence and is willing to try new things, but she takes care to protect herself by reducing some of the risk. Nevertheless, Yvonne's planfulness leaves some room for chance and improvising. When traveling alone, for instance, she always has reservations for her first night in any new place, as a guarantee, but from then on she prefers to make arrangements on the spot.

What is most salient about Yvonne is her energetic involvement. In her career search, she prepared actively by seeking *information* (books, workshops, advice from professionals and friends) and *support*. She found ways to use her contacts in imaginative ways, making the most of each interchange. As compared to Jules and Gary, Yvonne conducted a career search that was more deliberate and more concentrated. She also put a great deal of her own imagination into everything she tried to do. Thus, she did all the usual things—answering ads, pursuing networks, getting career counseling—but she did them in a special way. Along every major path she explored, she produced something of her own that showed acute sensitivity to the needs of her prospective employers: She drew up a list of questions for the nurses' association that caused its officers to go back to the drawing board and rethink their staff needs; she sent a critique of the women's magazine, with suggestions, to their central office; she wrote a proposal for a consultantship; she drew up a blueprint for the job she wanted at Goodwin's, and that blueprint—plus her obvious skill and persistence—caused them to create the job she had designed.

Yvonne not only was able to invest herself in everything she did, she also was able to invest *in* herself. She was willing to take the risk of using her resources to support herself through a transition period in a way that many people would find difficult; it was perhaps easier in her case because she had no one to support except herself—and her cat. Realizing that this was, indeed, the rainy day she had been saving for, she could allow herself to spend her money to buy time because of her conviction that she wasn't frittering away her resources but was actually underwriting herself and her future. It takes a fair degree of self-esteem to look at a period of unemployment that way and to give oneself permission to invest in oneself—to convert an *imposed* risk into a *chosen* one.

Three main lessons can be learned from Yvonne's experience. First, the most satisfying new careers are often those that allow you to tie together threads of past experiences and interests.

Second, once you have reached a certain age and experience level and a certain need for calling the shots, the best jobs are the ones you design or create yourself. This does not necessarily mean you have to be self-employed, only that your self must be fully employed.

Third—at a more general level—this tremendous investment in and of oneself is what enables people like Yvonne to look back and say—win, lose, or draw—"I gave my all." As my research has shown repeatedly, being able to say that turns out to be far more important than any given outcome in determining one's feelings about oneself as a risk taker.

A final point should be made about styles. Yvonne—who tends to worry like a Style A risk taker and to think more about the present and immediate future than about the past, like a Style C—gives mostly Style B responses. It's worth noting, however, that her risk-taking pattern isn't consistent or equally successful in all areas of her life. She told me, for instance, that, in a highly uncharacteristic episode a couple of years ago, she spotted an unusually attractive man "across a crowded room" (it was actually a restaurant) and suddenly found herself going up to him as he paid his check and saying to him, "I can't let someone with eyes like yours get away." (This "moment of madness" led to a year-long tempestuous relationship.) I mention this to show that even a consistent, orderly, balanced risk taker occasionally will behave totally out of character. Although people may correctly think of themselves as basically impulsive or controlled, security-minded or change-seeking, different areas and different circumstances may call out different responses.

Chapter 6
The Extremes of Risk Taking

> I think that it is useless to fight directly against natural
> weaknesses. One has to force oneself to act as though one
> did not have them in circumstances where a duty makes it
> imperative; and in the ordinary course of life one has to
> know these weaknesses, prudently take them into account,
> and strive to turn them to good purpose; for they are all
> capable of being put to some good purpose.
>
> Simone Weil, *Waiting for God*

In our discussion of risk-taking styles, we first looked at the three broad types
and then focused on six people who fall, with slightly different shadings, within
the large middle range—Style B, the balanced risk takers. In this chapter, I
will present the cases (partly composited, with all identifying details disguised)
of two people who, for at least part of their lives, operated at the extremes of
the risk-taking continuum: Meredith, who for a time lost the ability to risk, and
Paul, who for most of his life couldn't refuse a risk. Superficially, Meredith and
Paul are complete opposites. But in one sense they are very similar; for each,
the risk-taking process had become truncated or short-circuited through the
use of a single decision rule ("Reject all risk" or "Accept all risk").

I choose to focus on extremes at this point because they can function as
amplifiers to help us hear clearly the themes that are muffled in our own lives. I
will begin each case history by suggesting some issues to keep in mind, and I
will follow the two descriptions by exploring the risk-connected themes that are
highlighted in the histories of Meredith and Paul.

CASE HISTORIES

Meredith: A Woman Who Temporarily Lost the Ability to Risk

In reading about Meredith, we will consider these issues, among others: the
price one pays for acceding to too many imposed risks, one form of fear of
success and its impact on risking, and the ways in which a mother's pattern of

retreating from risk get repeated and varied in a daughter. The bell-shaped curve I presented in Figure 1 (p. 24) had sharply tapering ends, suggesting that few people choose to live at the extremes of risk taking. Toward the far left of the curve, we find people who cannot risk. Their fear of change is so great, their sense of danger and of their own power to do harm so omnipresent, that any move—like the slightest action of T. S. Eliot's J. Alfred Prufrock—may "disturb the universe." Different clinical types show this paralysis of action: those who are so profoundly depressed that they cannot muster the energy to act; those who are so anxious that they maintain a rigid, willed, intensely active, nonacting attitude; and those with phobias so strong that their fear of self-extension may spread to near-paralysis.

* * *

Meredith—an attractive, slender, 32-year-old woman with expressive blue eyes and a cap of curly, red hair—came to me because she was suffering from a deepening series of phobias that had begun a number of years earlier. In telling me of her situation, she sighed frequently and often shrugged and held out her hands as if to say, "Who cares?" or "What can possibly be done?"

At the point at which she entered therapy, her "panic attacks"—palpitations and feelings that her heart would burst—had reduced her to virtual immobility. She could no longer go to a restaurant with friends. She could not drive, and she could not ride in a car driven by anyone other than her husband. She could not enter large buildings. And for the previous few months, she could only with difficulty leave the house they had recently bought—the latest in a long series of moves dictated by her husband's career. Although she felt totally isolated in Orinda, their San Francisco suburb, and although she hated their new house, it had paradoxically become a sanctuary as well as a prison for her—hated but safe.

Meredith's desperation and her fierce will enabled her to keep her twice-weekly therapy appointments, and for the next two and a half years we worked together on the issues that underlay her panic and her immobility. In the course of the treatment, Meredith talked a great deal about her mother, who seemed to be ten feet tall and built of heavy metal. Even though Meredith now lived more than two thousand miles away from her parents' Chicago home, her mother was as present as if she were living with her (which, indeed, she was, having been allowed prominent and permanent tenure inside Meredith's head). Meredith's mother had gone into a profound depression at 32—Meredith's current age—when her second child, a son, was 2 and Meredith was 8, shortly after the family had moved into a new house. Meredith remembers her mother pining and refusing to eat, having periods of hospitalization when she would mysteriously disappear for what seemed like an eternity to the child. She remembers trying to stave off her mother's feared demise by making milkshakes and sweet desserts for her—the only food her mother would take. I commented on the terrible burden of being her mother's lifeline, and she acknowledged with a sigh that, indeed, it had been an overwhelming responsibility for an eight-year-old. Meredith's mother was extremely fearful but also very opinionated and controlling; she often appeared to control by fear. Her depression seemed to lift as if by magic or by a sheer effort of will after about four years.

Meredith described her father as a silent, psychologically absent man—an electrician who had wanted to be an engineer but had had to give up his aspirations in order to support his aging mother. "I think he never really wanted children," Meredith told me. Although his friends saw him as charming and affable, to the little girl at home he seemed abstracted—attending to her, when he did so at all, with annoyance. His defense against his wife's need to control was to give in just so far and then maintain a stubborn implacability.

In this construction of her early life (with all the biases such constructions always have, based as they are on the imperfect understanding of the child who experienced them), the only positive note Meredith sounded was the nurturance she received from her maternal grandmother—a warm and loving woman with whom Meredith stayed for days and sometimes weeks at a time.

As a child, Meredith did well in school and was placed in a class for the gifted. Although her mother has called her "a handful," she sees herself as having been a "model child." Even as an adolescent, she would only mildly rebel at her mother's rigid code. It was at about that time that she first experienced palpitations in response to strenuous physical activity. Later, the palpitations seemed to arise from and produce anxiety. Although all her cardiological examinations have been negative, when she is having an anxiety attack, the palpitations, her hyperventilation, and her feelings that her heart is about to explode have led her to believe she is going to die. She first had these symptoms acutely about nine years ago, after she had graduated from college, got a job as a secretary, and moved out of her parents' home and into her own apartment. The symptoms lasted about six months and then seemed to disappear as mysteriously as they had arrived.

After her panic attacks subsided, Meredith worked at increasingly demanding jobs in advertising and public relations. She describes herself as feeling very powerful during those days, tooling around Chicago alone as a young career woman, fearlessly taking buses home late at night without thinking twice about it. She loved being in the city (she had grown up in a suburb) and was "thrilled" by the canyons of skyscrapers in which her Loop office was located. She had friends, dates, and exciting work.

When she was 24 years old—about the age her mother was when she met and married her father—Meredith met Martin, a young graduate student who was working for his doctorate in biochemistry in Ohio and had come to Chicago over Christmas to visit his family. After a brief courtship, she and Martin were married, and she moved in with him in his apartment in Columbus. What she remembers about the wedding is that her mother arranged most of the details and that when Martin didn't like the kitchenware Meredith had chosen, she took it all back and let him choose what he wanted.

In Columbus, Meredith couldn't find a job writing advertising copy, so she became a secretary again—cleaning their small apartment and cooking at night, shopping on the weekends. Martin was too busy studying every night and weekends to help around the house at all. Meredith tried to keep cheerful, and, although she hated her job, she began to make a few friends. After a year and a half, Martin left school before writing his dissertation to take a teaching job in Massachusetts. Again, Meredith started as a secretary; again, she made a circle of friends. Because they stayed in Boston for four years, she managed to rise to a more responsible position in her agency, actually doing some administrative work and some copywriting, even though she was technically called "account assistant" (and the title rankled).

At about this time, the anxiety attacks returned; Martin was sympathetic and suggested that she have a cardiologist examine her; the results were negative. She thought fleetingly of getting psychological help, but her fear of "being crazy like her mother" and her mother's negative feelings about psychotherapy made her put it off.

She continued to hyperventilate, and gradually her fear took on more palpable forms. First she was afraid to ride in elevators; then she had to avoid tall buildings. Some days she was so anxious she literally couldn't get out of bed. But since her boss had colitis and was periodically laid up, they took turns "covering" for each other on the worst days.

Then Martin was awarded a research fellowship at a biological research institute in southern California—an opportunity too good to pass up, even though it meant another dislocation. In La Jolla, Meredith decided to take some courses in photography. This was the first time in her marriage that she had done something just for herself, and it was her happiest time. When Martin's fellowship was over and he took a research position at a hospital in San Francisco, it meant yet another move, saying goodbye to the close friends they—mostly Meredith—had made in La Jolla. This time, however, Meredith was moving with a real job in hand. A professor had recommended her to a major state official, who hired her as his part-time publicist/photographer. Although the work was sporadic, it was exciting and hectic. She had to make impromptu trips to the state capital in Sacramento, to stay overnight after late-night conferences, to meet emergency deadlines.

To Meredith, this personal success seemed to have come too quickly. Despite the kudos she had received for her work, she felt like a middle-aged beginner. And she was concerned about Martin, who said to her, half-jokingly, half-wistfully, "When you're a big, famous kingmaker, will you leave me?"

It was a few months after taking the new job and moving to Orinda that Meredith came to see me. By that time, her "panic attacks" had reduced her to immobility. Her life had become a parody of domesticity; confined to the house, she cooked elaborate meals, cleaned and dusted, and never touched her camera. She had, in effect, become her mother, although consciously she did not experience depression—only panic and concern that her life had ground to a halt.

She wasn't sure she could come to therapy twice a week, but "somehow" she managed that, faithfully, and we began to sort out the issues behind her symptoms. As she worked through them, her fears began to lift and shift, to become more contained and manageable.

To talk in terms of risk—at the time that Meredith came into treatment, she could no longer risk; furthermore, everything was a risk to her. A trip to the grocery store was like scaling Mt. Everest. Even a ride in a taxi could trigger the trapped feelings and the inability to breathe. As W. H. Auden wrote:

And the crack in the tea-cup opens
A lane to the land of the dead.*

*From "As I Walked Out One Evening," in *Collected Poems*, by W. H. Auden, edited by Edward Mendelson (New York: Random House, 1976), p. 115. Copyright 1976 by Random House, Inc.

Why could she not risk? Risk was synonymous with everything that was most terrifying to her in herself: ambition, aggressiveness, throwing her weight around, being a big shot, rising to the top. Meredith *wanted* success and power; at bottom she was ambitious, feisty, stubborn, even somewhat grandiose in her fantasies and aspirations. But she was terrified of these qualities, terrified that they would cut her off from her largely unconscious submission to her mother, who at the same age had suffered an immobilizing depression. Her fears were her badge of belonging to her fearful mother. Although Meredith's life was outwardly very different from her mother's, she was unconsciously bound not to supersede her. The retreat to the house in an endless round of cooking, cleaning, and dusting was an attempt to placate her mother-in-her-head by *being* that mother. It was also an attempt to reassure her husband, whom she deeply loved, by saying, "See, how could I possibly leave you? I can't even leave the *house* without you. Far from being the rising star you fear, I am a basket case. Without you I can't even move."

Her regression to the passive posture also hid Meredith's monumental anger: anger at her mother for her fearfulness and her control-by-illness; anger at her husband for having called all the shots—where and when they would move—in a series of uprootings that left her feeling lonely, always beginning over at new jobs and with new people.

In its acute stage, her agoraphobia, like most symptoms, represented a compromise between her unconscious desire and her defense against the forbidden impulse. So while she presented herself as helpless and paralyzed, she was in fact exerting tremendous control over her husband; for the first time in her marriage, *she* was calling the shots while getting off without blame. It was not she but "her illness" that "demanded" that Martin attend to her, stay by her side, help her.

During the course of the therapy, Meredith came to understand these things and to acknowledge her share in them. She came to see how her fear of being assertive not only had led her to *accept* Martin's whims and changes of heart but actually had fostered them. She learned that when she could say "Here I stand. I will not be moved" directly and not through a symptom, Martin would listen and respect her; that any act of resoluteness on her part was, in fact, welcomed by him.

She was increasingly able to acknowledge her impulses to power and success and to begin to modulate these impulses so that they took the form of realizable goals. Since she had found it harder and harder to work at photography, she decided, seemingly on impulse and at the recommendation of a friend, to take an insurance course and to study for the license.

Now—several years later—she is a successful insurance saleswoman. Her job requires that she do many of the things that would have seemed impossible several years ago: driving up and down steep hills, entering tall buildings, working 10- and 12-hour days, assuming more equality with her husband. Martin, it turns out, is mostly delighted (despite an occasional complaint about yet another late-night dinner). Her submission was partly to a phantom husband—not to the real man who, despite the derangements of routine and the greater demands on him imposed by her work, has enjoyed seeing her become vigorous and active.

Because Meredith's impulses to power and control were so intense and so deeply warded off, they often erupted in raw and blatant ways: fantasies about returning to photography someday and winning national acclaim, or confrontations in which this ordinarily gracious and beguiling woman would suddenly tell people off as though she were the Red Queen in *Alice Through the Looking Glass.*

The major task of the second part of her treatment was to modulate these extremes, to learn the terrain of appropriate aggression and integrated assertion. She came to see that each extreme was the reverse of the other, that the fear of being overwhelmingly big and powerful led to the retreat of being powerless. She came to see—and, more important, to *feel* with her whole person—that the choices were not between impotence and omnipotence but that she could find a way to be just ordinarily, humanly *potent.* Instead of taking no risks or taking foolish risks, she could choose risks that were appropriate to her age and stage and character and deepest needs, including the need to honor the people who are close to her. To the extent that selling insurance and making money at it are less heavily invested—less "hot" or self-defining than her photography was—she is able to take more risks with them. Perhaps one day she will have the courage to return to that important and neglected part of herself.

Meredith's Dream It often happens, among the dreams reported in the course of therapy, that one stands out as a vivid allegory of the patient's current psychological situation. Near the end of the therapy, Meredith described such a dream—a dream that had left her shaking and breathless:

> I was in a house. I don't know whose it was, but it wasn't any house I recognized. There was a door leading to the basement of the house, and I knew I had to go down there. When I got down, I found a small, white room in which there were two women—old women. They seemed to know who I was. They didn't have legs and were standing on stumps. They held out their arms to me, imploring me to stay. I was torn by indecision. I knew that, by leaving, I was abandoning them, and yet I couldn't join them.
>
> They began to wail, and it was almost impossible for me to turn my back on them, but I did it. I ran upstairs. And there was Martin, who seemed to be living in this house, too. I tried to tell him about the women, about the danger, but he didn't seem to take it in. He couldn't understand why I was so upset, why I had to leave. I finally said to him, "Look, we're going." And I pulled him out with me. I woke and my heart was racing and I just couldn't expunge the image of those two old, desolate women.

Dreams, we know, are susceptible to multiple levels and layers of interpretation. This was in part a dream about the therapy, about going down into the depths to confront the phantoms. It was also a dream about Meredith's ties to her mother and to that other disabled woman—the helpless, legless, impotent part of herself.

In associating to the dream, she remembered having visited a cemetery on her last trip to her parents' house, a cemetery in which her father's mother, for whom she had been named, was buried. "It was really spooky looking at the tombstone and seeing my maiden name on it," she said. The underground room thus seemed to be a mausoleum—in this case, a tomb for the *living* dead. Her guilt at leaving her mother and her mother-connected self was enormous. But leave she did. "And, you know," she said, "*they* could have left, too, on their stumps. The door was open. They were keeping themselves prisoners." She had become able to look at her fears, to name them, and to move on and out.

Meredith was able to see in this dream emblems of the major concerns in her therapy and in her life. These issues will claim our attention again after we consider the story of a man whose risk taking has the same all-or-nothing quality as Meredith's but in the opposite direction—that is, all, rather than nothing.

Paul: A Man Who Couldn't Stop Risking

In reading about Paul, we will see what can account for a person's compulsion to seek out risks, as well as the issues that may underlie a fear of failure and how they may be disguised and defended against. We will also note how a son's attitudes may be shaped by his parents' denial of anxiety and pain.

* * *

Paul came to see me shortly after the breakup of his six-year marriage, when he was in his late twenties and already launched in his law career. He had moved to California from Denver, Colorado, where he had grown up. A short, strikingly handsome man, with curly, blond hair and luminous, dark eyes, he appears somewhat fragile because of his slimness and an occasional stammer.

One soon forgets these emblems of frailty, however, as one watches the darting play of his mind. Paul is a rebel and an iconoclast. In law school, he repeatedly argued in class, almost always opposing the prevailing view expressed by professors or other students—even, he says, when he actually agreed with them! Fiercely competitive, he will work 30 hours on a brief that he could have written in 6 because he wants to build an absolutely foolproof case.

He uses explosive, scatological language (his colleagues are mostly "assholes" and "shitheads"), and he loves to shock. In his criminal law firm, he repeatedly asks for and gets the toughest cases—three-time losers, child molesters, hard-core addicts.

Paul came into treatment because he was feeling shaky and unable to cope after the breakup of his marriage. He had married young, following an intense, passionate courtship with a young woman (a musician) he had met while in college. After five years, their marriage had eroded from the constant fighting of two deeply caring but hot-tempered protagonists.

Paul knew when he entered treatment with me that there was a lot of material from his childhood that he needed to deal with. But he had wanted to "put all that away," not to exhume it. In fact, he told me, he had not looked at a single photograph of himself taken before the age of 14 because it was too painful. Paul had been born with hemophilia, which made him highly susceptible to injury and potentially fatal bleeding. For the first two years of his life, he was carried around on a pillow. He was so fragile that his mother had to be extremely careful in diapering him; the least twisting or pressure might cause him to bleed internally.

His eyes luminous with unshed tears, he said to me on his first visit, "You know those puffball fungi? The round ones you blow on and they disappear? That's how I secretly think of myself."

Paul's childhood was a mixture of illness, fear, denial of that fear, and counteraction. He has always been grateful that his parents sent him to public schools rather than special schools, even though it meant that he had to have special times to pass in his wheelchair, when the other children had already changed classes, so that no one would jostle him. Fire drills were nightmares. At the age of ten, when his condition seemed to improve and he was able to walk with braces, he insisted on roughhousing with his brothers. From early on, he began taking life-threatening risks.

Paul's parents (his father was a dentist, his mother a writer of children's books) encouraged him to ignore his disability. He came to realize in the treatment that they pursued this course out of fear and guilt as well as love and the desire to help him toward mastery. "My parents," he said, "gave me the message that I could be anything I wanted to be." "Even six feet four?" I asked him. He was taken aback at how desperately unrealistic some of his parents' fantasies were.

He remembers his father taking him to a ward of immobilized, quadriplegic children and saying, "See, you're not so bad off. Other kids have it much worse." As he recounted the incident to me, Paul became more acutely aware of how unempathic that presumably encouraging remark had been—how it made him feel that his own sense of himself as defective was something he had to conceal and bury.

As a result of his frequent injuries and respiratory infections, Paul spent much of his childhood in bed. During these hours of lying prone, Paul was ceaselessly active inside his head. He constructed elaborate fantasy worlds, made up games and languages, wrote and sketched. His mother, being a writer, encouraged this fanciful side of him—and, for most of his childhood, the two of them were very close. Clearly the favorite of both his parents, he was specially prized as the youngest, brightest, funniest, and most achieving among the family of three boys and a girl.

Paul's situation changed dramatically when he entered adolescence. For one thing, with newly developed medication and with the hormonal and physical changes of that period, Paul's medical condition almost miraculously improved and stabilized. For the first time in years, he could move about without imminent danger to his limbs. Some degree of fragility and joint swelling persisted. Basically, however, Paul was "sprung" into the world of adolescence as if released from prison.

At this point, as he put it, he "went haywire." Because he was so bright, he could get by in his high school by doing very little except cramming at the last minute. He cut most of his classes and experimented with marijuana, LSD, and psilocybin; he hung out with a much older crowd of writers and intellectuals in the nearby city. He learned to drive, and drove like a Manhattan taxi driver—plummeting down the serpentine roads in the Rockies way beyond the speed limit, "like playing Russian roulette on each curve." Whatever any of his friends was fearful of tackling, he would try. He spent one summer working in a pet cemetery, for instance, getting a grisly pleasure from his work. He also constantly risks offending others by compulsively joking about what is upsetting—such as dwarfs and paraplegics.

His image of his physical self was unrealistic. He knew objectively that he is small and slight; nevertheless, he had for years pictured himself to be well above average height, even though this perception actually requires that he ignore the kinesthetic experience of looking *up* to see many of his male friends. He was always surprised, when he glimpsed himself in a store window, to discover how slight he was; in the past, he had quickly obliterated that perception. He did that, in part, by "taking up a lot of psychological space"; in a group of people, he was constantly in motion—circulating, wisecracking, provoking, challenging. It made him feel big.

The issue of "big versus little" was highly focal for Paul (as it was for Meredith, who was troubled by the opposite fear—being too big). When his defenses failed, Paul had always experienced himself as fragile and evanescent. He was convinced that he would not live past 29 (an age that was only two years away when he entered therapy). Part of this conviction was based on the survival rates of untreated patients with his genetic disorder; part was the derivative of underlying feelings of hopelessness and insignificance. Indeed, his compulsive risk taking could be understood as a way to avoid inner anxiety and pain by projecting the danger onto the environment and seeking to master it there.

As a result, and out of an overwhelming need to deny his fear and his mortality, Paul had to do everything he could to prove he was *not* disabled. He would lift heavy furniture against doctor's orders. He would climb five flights of stairs instead of taking an elevator. He would make love three times a night, while his pulse was fluttering far beyond normal limits.

The reasons for Paul's continual risk taking were manifold and complex, but surely one of its sources was a fear of fear—the inability to admit his terror and thereby manage it in more adaptive, less life-threatening ways. To acknowledge the fear was to acknowledge everything about himself that he had strenuously tried to deny and disprove—that he was, after all, only a fragile puffball, vulnerable to the merest breath of wind. His fears of melting and disintegrating formed the subject of much of our work together, through which he finally was enabled to talk about his fears and nightmares of "turning into a blob—utterly without contour or solidity." He was afraid that the work of therapy would undermine this shell he had built around his fear and leave him exposed and uncontained, like a beached jellyfish.

In the course of the treatment, Paul became less afraid of lifting the lid, slowly and at his own speed; he came to trust me as an ally who would neither force him to look at his fears nor collude with his need to believe (as his parents had reinforced him to believe) that nothing was amiss. After six months of our work, he was able to look at the family albums in his parents' house and to actually *see* himself in those photos for the first time.

As we continued to work on the central big-little metaphor, he began to acknowledge for the first time both his physical smallness and the large psychological impact he had on his friends, his family, his colleagues, his clients, and his therapist. He recognized that this impact could be made not through his frantic activity and attempts to shock or disturb, but through his genuine wit and charm and his long-buried soft and compassionate qualities.

As a result, Paul increasingly came to value his life and to want to preserve it as long as possible. When a tumor in his left lung was diagnosed, he chose to go through with a dangerous operation in order to prolong his life, instead of writing it off as he might have earlier. True to form, he entered the hospital making jokes ("I asked the doctor if I would be able to ski after the operation, and he said I would. I said that was great, because I hadn't known how to ski before it."). He soon became the "mascot" of his wardmates—men in their fifties and sixties. In the valley of the shadow, he was still trying to deal with his fear by laughing it out of countenance. The operation was a success, and the tumor turned out to be benign.

Paul's Dream   Like Meredith, Paul reported a number of striking and important dreams; one of the most revealing was a dream he had shortly before he went for his surgery, about a year before the therapy concluded:

> In this dream there are two men. I'm not in the dream; I'm only the spectator. The two men are in a makeshift cabin in a desolate place, a desert. The wind whistles around it; everything is dry. One of the men is lying in bed; he's very ill, emaciated. He looks almost hollow, almost weightless; he's practically a skeleton. His eyes are glazed and feverish, and he's very weak. He can scarcely raise his head, and his breathing is labored.
> The other man is very different. He's sandy-haired, tall, and muscular. He looks like an athlete; he wears a T-shirt and trunks, and he's taking care of the sick man. It's not clear what their relationship is, but they seem to be very close. The strong man knows the sick man must have water or he will become dehydrated from the fever. There's an old rusty pump on the property, some little distance from the cabin. The strong man goes over to it with a bucket and he pumps and pumps. At first, nothing comes out, then a trickle. He carries it back to the cabin and gives it to his friend, who drinks it thirstily. Will he live? I don't know. The dream ends with the other one again back at the pump, still trying to draw out the water.

Again, the dream contains layers of significance: most immediately, anxiety about hospitalization, but also sexual themes, themes of relationship to the therapist as caretaker, and, once again, projections of aspects of the self. Despite—or, rather, because of—his denial ("I'm not in the dream; I'm only the spectator"), we can see the two men as representations of the split within Paul: the fragile invalid who yields to death and the potent coper who pursues life. But the dream suggests that this extreme division is inaccurate. The potent coper is not entirely potent (despite his frantic activity, he can only get a trickle from the pump); and the helpless invalid is not completely impotent—he does command the allegiance and the nurturance of the other one.

Everything about the dream is bleak—the isolation, the feverish patient, the nearly useless pump. Yet the issue is not resolved. It may well be that, through his strength and persistence, the stronger man can actually nourish and resuscitate the weaker one. In fact, Paul was resuscitated—both through the surgery and through the therapy. At 29, he was no longer setting survival limits or feeling that he was living on borrowed time; nor was he tempting fate by taxing himself senselessly. And he was beginning to heal the split in himself.

THE ISSUES FOR RISK TAKING: FEAR OF FAILURE, FEAR OF SUCCESS

What do these two case histories tell us? Meredith and Paul are in many senses "special." Statistically, the number of people with incapacitating phobias or self-limited infantile disorders is very small. But Meredith and Paul etch out motifs that are present more dimly and subliminally in many of us: the fear of success and the fear of failure; the fear of strength and the fear of weakness; the fear of assertion (perceived as aggression) and the fear of fear; the fear of being too big and the fear of being too small.

A person who cannot risk is someone who views action as aggression, whose unconscious rule is: By being active and powerful, you will hurt someone else. In Meredith's case, the most proximate target for such hurt was her husband, who, she imagined, could be injured by her getting too strong and independent. More distally and more deeply, however, the target was her mother. Again and again as a therapist I see people—usually, though not always, women—who experience being independent and powerful as a threat to the same-sex parent, particularly if that parent has been perceived as ineffectual, weak, depressed, or frightened. "Thou shalt not surpass thy mother" (or, for men, "thy father") is emblazoned on their inner shield. In one woman I know, it takes the form of bringing herself down every time she has scored some kind of victory in her work. Marge is a printmaker whose mother was very traditional; she "gave up her life" for her daughter and said, "I had my turn in the spotlight, now it's yours." When Marge is invited to exhibit her work, she immediately thinks of how humiliating it will be, how presumptuous she'll seem, how people will laugh at her. What she is doing is humiliating *herself* to scale down her pleasure in being important, in being noticed, in displaying herself—pleasure that is unconsciously equivalent to surpassing and ultimately destroying her mother.

In his paper "Some Character Types Met with in Analytic Work," Freud discusses a type he calls "those wrecked by success." He comments on the puzzling dynamic that causes people to collapse on attaining something they have long wanted—a marriage or a promotion. Among the literary examples he cites are two women, Lady Macbeth and Rebecca West (of Ibsen's *Rosmersholm*), both of whom rapidly decline just after they have achieved what they presumably most desired. He holds that the illness that occurs at the moment of accomplishment is motivated by guilt, that any success represents the original feared and wanted success—a victory in the Oedipal rivalry with the parent of the same sex. The present success presumably reconstellates that danger and that guilt.

Over the past decade, the whole notion of fear of success, especially in women, has increasingly captured the imagination of professional researchers and lay readers. A substantial amount of research in this area has flowed from Mattina Horner's 1968 doctoral dissertation on sex differences in achievement motivation and its expansion in her later professional and popular accounts. Attempts to refine and replicate her research have multiplied. The resulting literature is too complex, and its thrust too equivocal, to review here. An admirable survey of theories about the fear of success, as reflected in social anthropology, depth psychology, and imaginative literature, and a review of the relevant research are contained in David Tresemer's small and thoughtful volume, *Fear of Success*.

Tresemer asserts that the field has been characterized by interesting findings, with mixed successes in attempts to replicate. He discusses the methodological limitations of the typical attempts to use quantitative scoring based on simple response categories, but he adds that the concept of fear of success appears to be a central one, as personal and clinical experience and the nature of our myths testify:

> Real-life fear of success is far more serious than the level on which our measures have been working; to very many the concept has had great personal appeal, allowing them to organize previously unconnected personal experiences. When the research methods lag so far behind the richness of personal... idiographic meaning, it is time to change the research methods.

It would be a gross oversimplification to say that women are afraid of success and men of failure. We are all afraid of both to varying degrees, but the balance may be somewhat different in the two sexes. In his illuminating book, *Sex and Fantasy*, Robert May takes a stand that has become increasingly unpopular these days. May presents evidence for some genuine psychological differences between the sexes, particularly differences in fantasy patterns that emerge when men and women are given the same stimuli for fantasy production.* Given a picture of a man and a woman trapeze artist, for example, men tend to tell fantasies that recapitulate the Phaeton myth. (Phaeton was the presumed son of Apollo who persuaded his putative father to let him drive his chariot, only to get scorched by the sun and to fall.) These are stories of physical and emotional excitement, of undertaking a great and prideful risk and being vanquished in the attempt. Women, on the other hand, tend to tell stories that reembody the Demeter myth. (Demeter, the Greek goddess of earthly fruitfulness, retreated into mourning and quiescence when her daughter was seized by Hades, lord of the underworld, and she reawakened to new life when her daughter returned for half the year.) These are stories of loss and separation, of retreat followed by resurgence.

Thus, when men seek out danger, they may do so in part *because* they are afraid. May noted "the compulsively brave denial of all fear or hesitation and the vision of masculine toughness and determination that emerged in the interviews with men whose fantasy patterns are strongly in the male direction." Each sex, he suggests, defends against what might be called its contrasexual side (for Jungians, the *anima* in men, the *animus* in women). Thus women, so the argument goes, defend against their aggressiveness (often equated with striving, achievement, power, and masculinity), whereas men defend against fear (which is equated with weakness, with being passive and "feminine," with being absorbed into the primal, undifferentiated mother). These are themes we saw in heightened form in Meredith and Paul.

---

*Feminists or environmentalists will say, no doubt, that these differences are due to socialization. Until socialization patterns change remarkably, this may be a moot point. Nevertheless, May finds the characteristic patterns he notes even among young, "liberated" college women.

Again, these are relative differences. At bottom, nearly all of us are afraid—in different measure—of succeeding *and* of failing. Fear of failure is more obvious, more accessible, easier to talk about. We all know that failure is "A Bad Thing," that it causes pain and shame and loss of self-esteem. We tend to be less aware of the internal dangers of success. Or, if we *are* aware of them, we acknowledge them in an obvious, somewhat trivial form. Success carries certain demands or expectations; if you do well, you'll be expected to do as well or better in the future, and so on. But the more *subtle* dangers of success—the meaning of one's own success to the internalized parents and others we carry around in our heads—are harder to assess because they are farther from our everyday awareness.

In taking a risk, we engage both fears. If we fail, we will hurt ourselves; if we succeed, we may feel in our depths that we are hurting others. How can we steer between these dangers—the dangers of depression and of anxiety? How can we salvage self-esteem from our failures? How can we learn that our success need not threaten our ghosts—for that is what our internalized loved ones are? These are hard questions, and it takes hard work—often with help and support from others—to answer them. I will suggest some answers in the next chapter.

Part III
GETTING LAUNCHED

Self-Assessment Exercise 2: Response to Risk

Before reading Chapter 7, take a sheet of 8-½″ × 11″ paper and answer the following questions. You will find the chapter more meaningful if you can place your responses in the context of the research reported. Completing this exercise will also help you think some more about the issues involved in the risk-taking process to be discussed in Chapter 8.

Take a few minutes to think about a situation in your life in which you chose to face a major challenge—to do something that seemed both important and risky. Then answer the following in some detail:

1. What was the situation—the nature of the risk or challenge?
2. What did you feel you stood to gain or lose?
3. How did you feel at the time you undertook the risk?
4. How did you go about dealing with the situation? (Answer as specifically as possible.)
5. What was the outcome?
6. What feelings did you have about yourself as a result of how you dealt with the risk?

Chapter 7
Risk and the Sense of Self

> I discovered something important about falling by watching
> my baby learn to walk—the first real athletic feat that any
> of us perform. A baby is afraid, of course, but luckily he's
> not immobilized by his fear. He might be if he only
> knew, or remembered what his mother knows: how much
> it hurts to fall; in fact, he might never learn to walk,
> might decide that crawling's good enough. But a baby gets
> up on his hind legs and propels himself forward, happily
> unconscious of just how unsteady he is. A wobble is part
> of a baby's walk—it's what makes that walk so immensely
> touching—but it doesn't stop his determined forward mo-
> tion. Blessed are the wobblers, for they shall arrive.
>
> Chana Bloch, "Fear of Falling"

This is a chapter about wobbling and about arriving, but it is more about wobbling than arriving. I will emphasize, based on my own experience as a clinician and on the findings of research, that "getting there" not only is half the fun, it's what it's all about—the process is more important than the product. The process, wobbly as it is, is where good feelings about oneself come from.

WOBBLING: FEELINGS ABOUT TAKING RISKS

Anticipatory Feelings About Risk Taking

In Chapter 1, I spoke of an exploratory study I had conducted with 294 participants in workshops and courses on career change. These people also took the risk exercise that you completed just before beginning this chapter. A nearly equal percentage described feeling negative (48.5 percent) and feeling mixed emotions (44.3 percent) in preparing to make the risky change. The mixed feelings typically included such opposites as: "fear and determination," "sadness and attraction," "hurt and angry, but determined," "scared and excited," "excited and elated, but fearful." A very small percentage (6.5 percent) listed only positive feelings; among these 19 people, 3 actually had described a situation in which there was virtually no risk; of the remaining 16, 10 ended up with negative evaluations of themselves. This suggests that when you experience only positive feelings before taking a major risk, you are likely to default yourself at some point.

Outcomes of Risk Taking

Although the risk exercise was administered at the start of each conference or workshop, with no suggestion that participants pick risks that had been successful or unsuccessful, the large majority—71.5 percent—reported positive outcomes for their risks. Mixed outcomes were described by 15 percent and negative outcomes by 13.5 percent. What I want to emphasize here, however, is not that so many risks turned out objectively so well; more important is the finding that approximately half of those who described *unsuccessful* outcomes and nearly two-thirds of those who reported *mixed* outcomes nevertheless experienced *positive feelings about themselves* as a result of taking the risk. *Thus, simply deciding to do the risky thing was more self-enhancing than was any given outcome.*

Feelings About the Self

An overwhelming proportion of the 294 people—83 percent—said that they felt good about themselves ("more proud," "more confident," "I know I'm a survivor") as a result of embarking on the risky course they had described. Indeed, a fair number mentioned a carry-over effect; they felt that undertaking a difficult path had made or would make it easier to take another chance at another time. Slightly more than 11 percent of the respondents had mixed feelings about themselves afterward, often responding that they felt better about themselves on the whole but that old self-doubts continued to surface.

It is striking that only 5.5 percent—15 of the 294 respondents—felt bad about themselves subsequently. We already know that 10 of them were people who had experienced only hopeful, positive feelings at the inception of the risk. Later in this chapter, I will discuss the other infrequent circumstances in which taking a risk is connected with lowered self-esteem. In the meantime, we will look at the negative consequences for the self that arise from refusing a risk and from delaying or putting off venturing.

FEELINGS THAT STEM FROM REFUSING A RISK

A young man writes:

> In 1969 I decided to move from California to Alaska. I'd always wanted to go north and was excited at the idea of being able to do it. I was also frightened at starting a

new life—getting a job, making friends. I was dissatisfied with my present life and wanted a complete change. The move itself was not too difficult. I organized well and drove up there—almost turned around a few times but basically felt there was nothing much for me to return to, so I had to go on.

When I settled in Fairbanks, I found it was easier to make friends than I had expected and not difficult to find some job—delivering mail—but still very hard for me to really plan my life and get satisfaction out of what I was doing. I enjoyed the newness, the almost pioneer feeling of Alaska, but had a great deal of trouble with being isolated from the world "down there" and with the feeling that I was letting my life "just happen."

I ended up going back down after 8 months with the intention of returning to Alaska after some traveling. I never returned. My reactions varied. I felt very strong in having actually gone and survived the winter there. . . . I also feel that as a result of not being satisfied, I closed up and stopped taking risks—socially or physically. I have always felt unfinished because I ran and did not return.

In fact, this man did take a considerable risk, but he saw himself as running from the larger challenge he had set for himself. These feelings of incompleteness and of selling himself short have continued to distress him.

Such negative self-attributions are typical of people who see themselves as having refused or aborted a risk. A woman in her thirties, for example, describes quitting a dead-end secretarial job after a great deal of frustration; at first she resolved to look for something else, but panic set in, and she returned to her old job on a part-time basis, "where I stayed for two more years, feeling unable to move out and unable to commit myself to the job. . . ." (Shades of Gary, the probation officer who had such trouble quitting!) She experienced "lowered self-esteem due to failure to take any really decisive action. I felt I had compromised myself."

Another woman, a teacher with four children, ranging from kindergartner to teenager, decided to leave teaching, which she had been doing as a poorly paid, part-time substitute. She developed a good, functional résumé and began to feel really positive about herself and about finding a different kind of work. She went on several informational interviews, submitted her résumé, and then gave up at Christmas time, "because it took all my time and I needed to concentrate on Christmas for my husband and four children. I intended to continue later, but instead went back to substitute teaching again after Christmas." Although she continues to believe that her presence at home during her children's vacations and summers is important, she feels very discouraged about not having pursued the job change more vigorously. She concludes: "I guess I'm terribly afraid to fail. I let distractions or turndowns discourage me almost immediately."

FEELINGS THAT STEM FROM DEFERRING RISK TAKING

A small number of people in my study—mostly women—said that they had never taken a major risk in their lives, that, in fact, the career change or reentry they were contemplating in these workshops was the first major challenge they had ever initiated. This confession was usually accompanied by self-disparagement. But hopefulness issued from the feelings of finally beginning to take on a challenge. Typical of these responses is the following:

> I think I've avoided taking risks and taken the easy route instead—e.g., becoming a school librarian, postponing further career development in deference to time needed in raising children, moving with my husband's career changes, etc.
>
> Realizing that time is moving on, that I am responsible for my own choices, realizing that I have abilities I could be using to make myself feel productive and vital has led me to start searching for information to make better choices. I have in the past made choices which didn't require risks because I love security and success. It is scary and exciting at the same time to think of starting something new at 35.

Or this one:

> I feel, as many women must, that my risks have been "controlled." I went through school at an accelerated rate, and although I had major emotional responsibilities (my mother's death made me responsible for two younger brothers and a household) I went through life in a very narrow, no-risk way. I graduated from college, went into teaching, married, and when a family came along, stayed home.
>
> I now feel the other half of my life is *here* and *now*. I know I don't want to teach again, but I don't know if I can handle all the transitions and risks a new career will entail. This is the challenge I'm facing at this moment. And I wonder if I have the experience to be able to meet it.

Two motifs have figured in these responses of people who have refused or delayed taking risks: (1) *fear*—particularly the fear of failure; and (2) *a questioning of competence* in taking responsibility for one's life course. Both these attitudes have hampered their risk taking and have ultimately lowered their self-esteem. I will examine both of these themes more carefully.

FEAR: WHEN IS IT ADAPTIVE AND WHEN MALADAPTIVE?

As psychologist Neal Miller has pointed out, the important question is not "Am I afraid?" but "What have I been motivated to *do* in a fearful situation?" Miller says that "fear can motivate either withdrawal or instrumental action." Fear of driving can cause us either to stay off the road or to buy insurance and drive carefully. The idea that fear is not necessarily maladaptive is suggested by a study cited by Miller in which Air Force officers reported on how they performed in relation to the degree of their fearfulness. There was some disagreement about the effects of strong fear—34 percent saying they did better and 25 percent saying they did worse when very fearful. But nearly half the officers (49 percent) said they performed more efficiently under *mild* fear. We also know from a host of studies of human and animal learning that some degree of emotional arousal—whether through anxiety or bodily needs, such as the desire for food or sex—is necessary for efficient functioning. If we exceed the optimal amount, performance drops off; but anxiety itself is not necessarily harmful.

Anxiety's effect on performance depends not only on the degree of anxiety but also on what we have learned to do when we are anxious. Physiologically, fear trips off either of two opposite patterns of responding. One is the flight-or-fight pattern: increases in heart rate and in activity level and, in animals (and sometimes in humans), loud and anguished vocalization. The other pattern is freezing, stopping all activity, remaining mute—even, in some cases in animal studies, feigning death.

Although we cannot draw absolute conclusions from animal studies, we can certainly regard them as suggestive. Miller describes a study by J. M. Weiss in which pairs of rats in separate soundproof boxes were wired together by the tail, so that each member of a pair received the same strength of an electric shock. Half the rats were taught a coping response to the shock: when the shock was turned on, they were taught to jump onto a platform to escape the shock. The control animals were given the same amount of shock but no coping responses. When the brains of the rats were analyzed, Weiss found that the brains of the coping-response rats showed elevated levels of nor-epinephrine, while the helpless rats showed decreases in brain norepinephrine. We do know that when depressed people are treated with antidepressant medication, their brain norepinephrine increases. The less helpless rats were thus less "depressed" (whatever that means in the mental life of a rat) than the more helpless ones.

Miller concludes that these laboratory studies confirm what we already know from a host of clinical studies on helplessness and depression—that *learning to cope while afraid* is very important. He goes even further:

> The results on the increase in norepinephrine levels suggest that there may even be some psychological advantage from meeting and successfully coping with a manageable stress of fear. In the complete absence of stressful challenges, some of the joy of life may be lost.

Another suggestive study by Weiss again took pairs of yoked rats in separate soundproof boxes and again subjected them to the same level of electric shock. In this case, however, one member of the pair received a tone as a signal of the shock before it came, but the other didn't. On autopsy, the nonsignaled group was discovered to have many more stomach lesions than the signaled group. The animals that were signaled had produced only intermittent fear responses—in response to the tone. The unsignaled animals apparently lived in fear all the time; they couldn't turn the fear on and off when appropriate. This study suggests the importance of reducing fear through preparation and by focusing it, so that continual, free-floating anxiety doesn't take the place of the highly specific, manageable fear of a particular thing at a particular time.

In making a major life change, we are afraid of two basic classes of outcomes: loss and failure. Fear of loss is appropriate because it causes us to reckon with—and to mourn—what we may be giving up: people, places, goods, status, known routines, the approval of others, and the sense of continuity that I talked about in Chapter 2. We don't—and shouldn't—jettison these lightly. But fear of failure is something else—often something far less rational—and this is what we need to look at now.

FAILURE AND THE FEAR OF FAILURE

What are we afraid of when we fear that we will fail? Most often, we are afraid of how we will appear to others: "I'll look stupid," "I'll make a blithering idiot of myself," "I'll be ashamed." If we were to "fail" at something without anyone else's knowing about it, would it bother us so much? If we could shed this need to preserve a certain image, then perhaps we could look at "failure" in quite another way.

You'll notice that I have put the words *fail* and *failure* in quotation marks. I do this to emphasize that our definitions of failure are generally relative and highly subjective. I am not talking about persistent, repeated, intractable patterns of failing. These bespeak either some need for punishment—often unconscious—or some gross lack of fit between our standards and our performance. (William James held that self-esteem equals the ratio of our successes to our pretensions, that is, to our expectations. If our expectations are unrealistically high, almost any outcome will feel like a failure and will lower our self-esteem). I am talking about the failures *most* of us experience—the garden-variety failures that are sprinkled among the successes of our lives.

In talking about these ordinary failures, it may help to highlight the issues by looking at the more extreme cases in which the themes are amplified. A consideration of clinically depressed people—those who are most preoccupied with their felt sense of failure—can provide a clue to what we can learn about ourselves and our own self-judgments.

In his very useful book, *Depression,* psychiatrist Aaron Beck writes of the distortions that depressed people impose on their world and of the skewed notions they have about their own achievement. First, the standards of depressives are excruciatingly high, so that any minor deviation from perfection seems to them to equal total failure. In other words, their tolerance range for what is good enough is very narrow; it is virtually a single point (perfection), rather than a *range.* A depressed high school student who does moderately well but fails to make the honor roll thinks of himself as "an academic failure." A depressed businessman who, after a string of successes, makes one money-losing transaction, thereafter becomes plagued with the idea that he is "completely stupid."

In addition to having cripplingly high standards, depressives tend to exaggerate others' negative responses to them. A depressed woman who is courteously asked by her boss to correct some errors in a report will say that she was really "chewed out" and "made to feel like a failure." Any criticism is perceived as a deadly attack. Furthermore, any neutral or descriptive comment addressed to them is seen as a negative judgment. I once told a depressed patient that he had a hard time allowing himself not to worry, and he responded, "So you must think I'm a bad person."

The other side of the coin, as we know from clinical and experimental evidence, is that depressed people generally and systematically *underestimate* their own success.* Beck cites a telling study in which he and his co-workers asked 20 depressed patients and 20 nondepressed people, matched for age and sex, to perform a routine card-sorting task. The depressed people not only gave more pessimistic predictions of how they would do, but, even more important, when they had completed the task, they underrated their actual achievement. Although their overall performance was not significantly different from that of the nondepressed control subjects, they rated their own performance more poorly than the control group rated theirs.

Tempering Perfectionism

Such data suggest that, even among people who are not clinically depressed, at least some of their so-called failures have to do with perfectionism: setting goals unrealistically high and rating achievements unrealistically low.

How can we shift our frame of reference about "failure" to reduce its negative consequences? The first step is to examine our perfectionism. In my clinical work, I have observed that people often are highly unaware of the assumption that they carry around with them and tacitly operate under—that unless they do a particular task "perfectly" (or, indeed, unless they themselves are "perfect"), they are doing poorly.

I am not suggesting that we should celebrate slipshod performance and lack of standards. In fact, the assumption that departing from perfectionism means espousing shoddiness is itself a fallacy born of the perfectionist idea that there is only one right solution and that everything else is inadequate. We all know that commitment and dedication to our life tasks are essential. What we must examine from time to time is the nature and quality of this dedication—its suppleness, its appropriateness. This brings to mind two executives I know— both immensely gifted and intelligent people. Brian is a workaholic who invests himself totally in everything he does. But because he operates on the assumption that he stands or falls with his every action, with every piece of

---

*Drawing on the "learned helplessness" research of Martin Seligman, more recent studies (for example, the work of Carol Diener and Carol Dweck) have shown that depressed or helpless children and adults estimate their success rate as distortedly low; other studies (especially the work of Lauren Alloy and Lyn Abramson) have suggested that depressed people actually are more accurate, whereas so-called normals may have a protectively *inflated* view of their own performance. In any case, realistically or not, people who are depressed do rate their own performance lower than nondepressed people do.

paper that leaves his desk, he is constantly checking out his "achievement Dow-Jones" (How am I doing? Is my stock rising or falling? How do I look to others?). At the same time, he cannot delegate work because he doesn't trust anyone else to do it as scrupulously as he would.

Barbara, on the other hand, is able to take a more distanced view of her own functioning. She sets priorities—almost automatically—so that she is able to give her all to one project but let go of the less important ones, easily delegating them to people whose competence she allows herself to trust.

Perhaps *letting go* is the key term here. Letting go of your zeal for perfection is letting go of a little part of yourself. But that, in turn, requires a certain security about who you are; if you're uncertain about that, you can't afford to relinquish anything. Letting go means having confidence that whatever you do is "good enough" and that "good enough" is really all that fallible humans can aspire to. Only saints, romantics, and seekers of omnipotence require perfection.

Many of us, alas, have not learned that lesson. Everywhere we see the "supermoms" who are trying to be everything to their children while at the same time running their homes smoothly and, in recent decades, holding down demanding jobs. Such demands—some of them self-imposed—are guaranteed to make one feel like a failure nearly all the time. How much more appropriate is the notion developed by British psychoanalyst Donald W. Winnicott—the idea of the "good enough" mother. This goal is within the grasp of most mothers. There *is* an alternative to being the perfect, empathic, ever-attentive mother (whose omnipresent attention and understanding would make it impossible for the child to separate, disengage, and see the mother as the Other). That alternative is not being a neglectful or cruel person, but rather being a mother (or, sometimes, a father or a mother substitute) who is reasonably sensitive and reasonably good at judging the child's needs and who will, inevitably, make mistakes.

When mothers of my generation were bringing up our children, the "bible" was Benjamin Spock's *Baby and Child Care.* When our one-year-old son fell out of his crib on his head, the first thing my husband and I did after checking him was to run for Spock, which contained reassuring words to the effect that "any child who hasn't had a fall by the time he's a year old is probably being too closely watched."

Our perfectionism as parents may inhibit the growth of our children. They may learn from our mistakes; and *we* may learn from our mistakes. Taking a leaf from Spock, we can say, "A life that hasn't had a bad fall is being too narrowly lived." In fact, as we saw from the case studies in Chapters 4 and 5, it is almost always a setback or a difficulty that forces us to change. Growth is born in pain and brings the risk of further pain. A patient once said to me, despairingly, "As soon as I get life under control, something happens." What happens is life—a process that refuses to be put under control and refuses to yield to our notion of perfect order, perfect harmony, perfect anything.

Learning from "Failure"

We must not only temper the perfectionism we all have to some degree, we must actually reframe our notion of failure—seeing what it can do *for* us as well as *to* us. This kind of rethinking or reframing is like twirling a kaleidoscope: the pieces are still the same; all that changes is the relationship among them. But that change of configuration can make all the difference. A new pattern has new meanings.

Thus, we are permitted—perhaps required—to think of failure not as something to be dreaded but as something we can *use*. Here we can get some guidance from people in the performing arts. What they do is so self-revealing, so self-exposing, that it highlights the issues raised in most major risks. I know two musicians who are married to each other—the woman an oboist, the man a pianist. Each describes feeling the same symptoms before a concert: heart palpitations, sweaty palms, rapid breathing. The woman labels these symptoms "stagefright"; the man has learned to call them "excitement." By relabeling these sensations, he reduces his anxiety and experiences it for what it truly can be—an aid to performance.

Actors know this very well. One of the perils of playing in a long-run show is that the anxiety of the first few nights is dissipated, and the actor settles on a safe, unfocused performance, aiming for effects. Jon, an actor who also teaches acting, once said to me, "I used to be afraid of my anxiety. Now I know how much it does for me, how much it enforces concentration and energizes my work. So when I start feeling anxious, I hail my anxiety as a friend. 'Hi, there, anxiety, old pal,' I say to myself, 'what can you do for me today?'" The successful professional is someone who has learned not to fear his fear but to use it constructively. As one teacher put it, "It's not a bad thing to know that I'm unsure and to teach anyway. The teaching is more likely to be alive."

The teacher who said that is craftsman-philosopher Carla Needleman, and her small, profound book, *The Work of Craft*, is the most cogent account I have read about the usefulness of failure. Drawing her metaphors from a variety of crafts, but especially from pottery, she explores what can be learned about crafts as a means of self-knowledge and about the relationship of self to process—to making, shaping, succeeding, and failing.

Needleman sees the need for success as "a constrictive force that bars me from immediate participation in the moment as it appears, prevents the all-important conversation with the material of craft," by forcing a focus on product or end point and thereby neglecting the flow of process. She sees the need for success and the fear of failure as two sides of the same coin: "For it isn't failure that causes the sinking sensation we all know but the fear of failure. Failure isn't the enemy, fear is. We learn, after all, by failing."

She goes on to give an example of her first concentrated attempt to make—in her terms, to "study"—a plate. At first, she says, everything went wrong—her plates were too flat; later, they were too sharply indented. "Each plate," she says, "was a failure, and each failure drew my interest more and more. I became less interested in making plates and more interested in how the learning process proceeds in me."

Eventually, Needleman produced a series of perfect plates, but she felt that, because of the sweated labor that had gone into them, they just didn't look "happy":

> I would not accept these plates as a success. I insisted on my right to take them as failure because I wanted to go on. Success is a destination. One gets off the train and has to find something else to do. I was too interested to stop yet.

To see success as a dead end and the way of failure as a way of learning—a beginning point—requires that we stand our values on end. But if we can do that, the dividends are enormous, since all of us "fail" in some ways more than we succeed. Indeed, in the most ultimate sense, as novelist John Fowles has written, "All of us are failures; we all die."

If we reframe our idea of failure as something to be used rather than avoided, we can say, with Carla Needleman: "The more I can bear to risk to fail, the more, like Antaeus, contact with the earth will renew my life." Antaeus, you may remember, was a wrestler in Greek mythology who was invincible so long as he touched Mother Earth. In this metaphor, failure drives one back to the nourishing matrix inside the self that enables one to try again.

Regarding success as a dead end, and insisting on one's "right to fail" may seem paradoxical and perverse. It certainly represents a 180-degree turn of the kaleidoscope from the perspective we usually have—our dogged determination to succeed and our wish to avoid failing at almost any cost. But what a liberating reversal it is when we can believe, in our deepest selves, that we are free to release into the process of living as a process of learning without being tied to the rack of outcome. Perhaps you are complaining, "Well, that's all fine so long as you're doing something like making a plate. But what about a really high-risk enterprise such as making a marriage or making a new work life for myself? Can I have such a detached, Olympian perspective then?" The answer, obviously, is that it is much harder when "hot" cognitions and life-threatening choices are involved. Even there, however, we can learn by patiently reminding ourselves that there is another way to look at mistakes and another way to approach challenges.

RISK TAKING AND SELF-ESTEEM

It *is* harder to deal with our mistakes in the big life changes we have talked about in this book. Even in taking large risks, however, we can "fail" in some objective sense and still regard ourselves and the undertaking as worthwhile. That is what makes it possible for 50 percent of the subjects in my study who reported negative outcomes to their life changes to say that they nevertheless felt good about themselves. And it is why *none* of those who refused a risk or retreated from one felt pleased.

The good feelings that result from taking a risk—even one that does not turn out as hoped for—are of two sorts: (1) seeing oneself as a survivor and (2) learning about oneself in the process.

Seeing Oneself as a Risk-taking Survivor

Undertaking a difficult life decision can contribute to an expanding image of oneself as someone who prevails. In *How People Change*, psychiatrist Allen Wheelis has written that just as action can follow insight (the usual therapeutic model), so insight can follow action; sometimes we learn who we are through doing. Wheelis goes further by asserting that we actually become who we are through doing: "We are what we do." The thief who refrains from stealing in every situation in which he is tempted is no longer a thief. The timid person who forces himself or herself to take one risk, and then another, is eventually a risk taker. Taking one risk doesn't do it, but it is a step, and my research shows that it is accompanied by an expectation of continuity: "Next time it will be easier. I can draw on the 'credit' of my behavior this time." Here are some typical examples of this feeling:

> *A woman who traveled alone after separating from her husband.* As a result of this experience I had a real feeling of my own power as a coping person—one who is able to take reasonable risks and deal successfully with new situations. I felt much more independent than at any other time in my life, and I loved it. The feeling of self that I brought home with me from my trip helped me to deal more effectively with my other life situations, and I still look back on that experience when my self-confidence starts to slip. Having done it once, I know I can achieve those feelings again.

> *A young man who tried out for the boxing team, risking being beaten up in the ring:* I lost the fight, but in spite of it I was glad I went through with it. I actually was a happier person and felt that I had accomplished something and would try other things.

> *A young woman who traveled to Nashville to cut her first record:* The record wasn't that good, but I am still trying. . . . I am proud of what I've done so far. . . to go and try something I had wanted to do all my life.

> *A woman who moved to be with a new man after a divorce:* There was pain and discomfort in the beginning. But I'm proud that I was flexible enough to take a risk and not know the outcome. My feelings of competence and ability to control my own life increased. I no longer feel I'm run as much by the circumstances of my life.

The emphasis in all the foregoing accounts, and in the typical responses, is on *mastery*—on the amount of control one can continue to exert in an ambiguous or difficult situation. Mastery can be gained whether the outcome is "successful" or not, as we noted in the example of the man who lost the fight and the woman who cut the unsuccessful record. Here is a more fully described example of a risk that failed in one sense but not in a more basic one:

> In 1975 I had reached a stage of growth professionally that increased my dissatisfaction with the public school system in which I had worked 18 years. Together with two colleagues, I embarked on a venture designed to convince our district that alternative schools based on learning styles were needed if we were ever to motivate kids in a positive, exciting way. After several successes (we actually made an end run around one department and ran two seminars in our in-service programs), we were told to stop our campaign and be quiet, like good, naive, sweet little teachers.
>
> I now saw myself on the brink of a decisive step. I could return to my classroom, shut the door, and create a good learning environment for the kids who took my courses, or I could say "shove it" and look for another job. When you're in your forties and have been raised on the notion that job security is priority number one, this type of decision can be devastating. Nevertheless, I decided to take the plunge.
>
> I wrote 45 letters to various alternative schools throughout the country and got 45 warm replies, but also 45 rejections. It was 1975, and alternative schools were in trouble.
>
> Suddenly I was offered a job in a neighboring town—to be principal of a new secondary school and help create it from scratch. I slept little for several weeks, but I decided to take the plunge. I resigned from Neanderthal Land and set out to humanize a public school system.
>
> Two years later, boxed in by an ignorant Board and a newly hired idiot administrator, I am convinced that humanistic change in the system is unachievable. I am once more ready to look for something else in which to invest my talents and interests.
>
> The fear is still with me—but I work hard at tuning in to my own center of inner strength, and I am convinced that my choice two years ago was right and helped me to grow as a person. Life is now exciting and unpredictable, and I have faith that I will continue to move and grow and that change, however frightening, must always be a part of my life.

Learning About Oneself

We not only can reaffirm ourselves in risk taking but we also can learn about ourselves, even when we "fail." Of course, we can learn from our successes, too. But the lessons we learn from our failures are sometimes more precious, because they are more painfully earned and more sharply etched.

Learning from experience not only means learning how—how we behaved wisely or how to do it differently the next time—but, equally important, it means learning *who we are*, finding out things about ourselves that we might not have discovered if we hadn't attempted the difficult unknown. This is what Needleman means by learning through "the way of failure."

What do we learn about ourselves through risking, even—perhaps especially—if we fail? We learn about our true values, our styles, our coping skills, our needs, our sticking points, and our bottom lines. Consider the following comments:

A woman writes of her decision to accept a demotion from administrator to classroom teacher following a systemwide cut in funds:

> I approached it with great hesitancy because of the blow to my self-esteem and because I wondered whether I could relearn all the old teaching skills, relearn to read kids and enjoy their development on a day-to-day basis.
>
> Not only did I learn these again, but I also learned something about myself. I know now that I am more comfortable and happy working with people cooperatively than administering or telling people what to do or how to do it.

A man who took on a huge community organization effort for a political initiative campaign in a distant community writes:

> The outcome was frustrating. Overcoming community resistance to me as an outsider, dealing with small-town gossip, and running into hostility were difficult. The initiative was defeated 2 to 1. But three years later, the attitude changed greatly. And I learned from this experience that there is truly a time to "let go" and move on.
>
> I paid a price for learning what I did, but the knowledge about working with others and my own strengths and weaknesses is worth everything.

A woman tells what she learned through an only half-successful attempt to reenter the work force after ten years at home with young children. Her search caused her to take further training, but the job she eventually found was still below her qualifications. Despite her discouragement, she could still feel she had learned a great deal about herself that was worth knowing:

> I learned that:
>
> (a) I'm a perfectionist.
> (b) I've been very successful in my work in the past.
> (c) I have a strong fear of failure.
> (d) I'm a lousy risktaker.
> (e) I'm trying to cope with c) and d) so that I can maximize the pleasure and challenge I could get from a new career alternative at this point in my life when I look forward to 20+ more years of working.

A man who felt burned out and quit his job as a draftsman, with no other job in the offing, was unable to find a similar position, became ill, and ended up taking a job he didn't like:

> In retrospect, I could have done a lot more thinking about my overall potential likes and dislikes. I discovered more about who I was. I discovered more fully my strengths, and that I can and do take risks in crucial situations. It was a very bad time, yet it was a learning experience. Weighing all that, I would do the whole thing again, but a little differently this time.

A woman applying for the position of project director in an organization where she had recently applied and been turned down for a similar post comments:

> Applying for this other position meant confronting the fact that I again might be turned down by the same people. I prepared for the interview as best I could, put a lot of energy into the resume, and although the position is still open, I'm quite sure I won't get it.
>
> The challenge was—and is—multileveled. Although I'm in a secure position in the company, the challenge to advance involves self-esteem and learning (a long, slow process) that "no" doesn't mean I'm less capable or worthy than I am. It means learning that the real world is "a tough cookie" and that if I'm going to provide the richest, most fulfilling life for myself, I need to keep sticking my face in the wind.
>
> In short, it means working hard to redefine "failure," what rejection feels like, and how to proceed with an embarrassed, slightly scared face.

In the course of living, how do we learn about ourselves? We learn when we react in a different way to an old situation, seeing new connections, or when we test ourselves by placing ourselves in a new situation. Risk taking, *by definition*, means exposing ourselves to the unknown. Therefore, it produces a forced growth, because it calls on skills, talents, and perceptions that we have not used in the same way before. It arises from the need for competency or mastery, which many psychologists believe to be a uniquely human drive that sets us off from other species with whom we share our other, "tissue" drives (for food, water, sex).

The urge to risk reflects the urge for competence; rightly approached, it can enhance that sense of competence, which is so intimately connected with self-esteem. As psychologist Stanley Coopersmith wrote in *The Antecedents of Self-esteem:* "The individual with high self-esteem feels capable of coping with adversity and competent enough to achieve success, and. . . the individual with low self-esteem feels helpless, vulnerable, and inadequate."

The matrix for these feelings is laid down by our early experiences, particularly in our relations with our families; but later experiences, though perhaps not so decisive, can neverthless serve to cement or erode self-esteem. If we learn that active responding produces reward or relief, we're likely to pursue that pattern. If we learn that responding doesn't make much difference, we soon stop trying. The pattern of "learned helplessness" that is associated with depression has been demonstrated in both human and infrahuman organisms. Remember the rats who learned that they could use their own responses to escape painful shock? Their behavior was far less disrupted than was the behavior of the rats for whom the shock was terminated by the experimenter's response rather than by any action of their own.

In deliberately taking a risk, we are voluntarily exposing ourselves to a series of possible shocks. This makes us understandably anxious. Usually, we can turn off or at least reduce the shock by our own behavior. But if we fail to move, or if we can salvage nothing from the slings and arrows to which we have exposed ourselves, we end by being depressed. Anxiety and depression—our lives represent a constant oscillation between these poles. If we can learn the appropriate responses to reduce the anxiety and to learn from the danger, we may then be able to say, in a variant of Hotspur's metaphor, "out of this nettle, danger, we pluck this flower, self-worth."

When Risk Taking Is Associated with Self-Disparagement

You will remember that, in the sample I studied, virtually all those who refused a risk ended up feeling bad about themselves. Conversely, only 5+ percent of those who had pursued their risk were self-disparaging.

In looking over their responses, I discovered that there were three major causes for these few instances in which lowered self-esteem followed risk taking: (1) internalizing bad luck, (2) failing to internalize success, and (3) self-reproach because of lack of preparation.

The first two of these sources have to do with the appropriate assignment of responsibility: neither claiming responsibility for what is truly outside one's control nor refusing responsibility for what is within it. If you have done most of the right things in attacking a life challenge and find it has turned out badly, you may appropriately feel sad or frustrated or discouraged about the outcome—but *not* about yourself.

Conversely, if you have had a success, you ought to be able to claim credit for the part of it that was not due to luck or chance. But some people— particularly those with depressed or masochistic tendencies—find this hard to do. This tendency to pluck defeat from victory is characteristic of people with chronic low self-esteem or fear of failure. They often attribute their failures to their own limitations while seeing their successes as due to flukes or to chance.

One woman in my group, for example, described the risk of speaking before an audience of 3500 people:

> I was terrified at the thought of speaking in public. My fear was that I would forget what I had to say, jumble my thoughts, stutter, and commit any of the other fantasies where I make a public fool of myself.
>
> I felt panicky: dry mouth, rapid heartbeat, excitement, dread, and the hope that the need for me to speak would evaporate.
>
> Sheer emotion and crowd dynamism carried me through. I calmed down, the 3500 people became faceless, and I did my speech.
>
> The outcome was overwhelming acceptance. I felt joy and pride, but then I have told myself that the success was because of external circumstances: emotional level of the audience, the subject, and the receptivity of the audience to what I had to say. I was in the right place at the right time.

Note that she cannot *own* her success in any way but attributes it entirely to external circumstances. This kind of skewed attribution—"my failures are my own, my successes are due to luck or circumstance"—is a very powerful way of keeping oneself down. A more realistic assessment would acknowledge the "rightness" of the circumstance while adding into the equation one's own contribution.

The first two tendencies I have mentioned give rise to low self-esteem through misattribution of the agency of the self: claiming blame when it is inappropriate, refusing credit when it *is* appropriate. The third tendency is more realistic—an assessment that is concerned not so much with a global good or bad judgment but with understanding the specifics of what went wrong. Indeed, 10 of the 15 people who felt worse about themselves after taking the risk pinpointed the source in this way; they felt they either had prepared insufficiently in taking the risk or had been excessively optimistic, which may be a special case of insufficient preparation. We noted earlier that people who described only positive anticipatory feelings were more likely to feel bad afterward than were those who had negative or mixed anticipations. In short, people who had not sufficiently canvassed alternatives, who had leaped in despite severe misgivings, or who had leaped in *without* misgivings were the ones who felt the experience had been ego-damaging.

The kind of preparation necessary to forestall such damaging self-imputations is learnable and teachable. It forms the crux of Stages 3 and 4 in the risk-taking process, as we shall see in the next chapter.

Here I want to reemphasize that the feeling of "I goofed!" need not be an end point but can be the stimulus for beginning a new process—a process of exploration that transforms an end-point evaluation (good/bad) into a feedback loop for further activity (How can I do it differently next time?). This is because *risk is a process, not an outcome.* You don't get only one chance. If you foul up, you can fix it up. This is what makes a continuing life. The man who said, "As soon as I get things under control, something happens," had a utopian and static view of the universe, as if one could ever halt the flow of change. Emphasis on perfect outcomes overlooks the continuity of change and the continuity of opportunity to shape that change.

Chapter 8
Stages in the Risk-Taking Process

> If...one's destiny is shaped from within, then one has
> become more of a creator, has gained freedom. This is
> self-transcendence, a process of change that originates in
> one's heart and expands outward, always within the pur-
> view and direction of a knowing consciousness, begins with
> a vision of freedom, with an 'I want to become...,' with a
> sense of the potentiality to become what one is not. One
> gropes toward this vision in the dark, with no guide, no
> map, and no guarantee. Here one acts as subject, author,
> creator.
>
> Allen Wheelis, *How People Change*

How does one go about taking a personal risk successfully? What stages must
one pass through to emerge at the end feeling better about oneself? This
chapter will spell out the essential components of the process. We must not
think of these stages as unvarying sequences in a fixed timetable (like
the maturational changes in childrens' motor development or Piaget's cognitive
stages or Erik Erikson's stages of psychosocial development). The stages may
not occur in the precise order mentioned, and, indeed, we may have to pass
through some of them more than once in any particular risk. We may, for
instance, experience ambivalent feelings (Stage 3) even while or after we are
attempting to reduce the risk (Stage 4).

In other words, what follows represents a roughly chronological index of
the steps one must take in launching a major life change. If we totally omit any
of them, we may end up in trouble. People who have different risk-taking styles
will need to focus more intensely on particular aspects of this process to help
correct for their specific bias, as I shall indicate later in the chapter. Because
this is a psychological analysis, I will emphasize feelings and ideas as much as—
perhaps more than—overt actions. A large part of the preparation for any major

change takes place inside our heads, and our success depends very much on the messages we give ourselves as we traverse the unknown territory of our risk. You will note that I have chosen to label the stages with verbs rather than nouns. I mean to emphasize thereby that risk taking is a process, not an end point. We talk of steps or stages, but it would be more correct to think of activities, especially if activities are taken to include the internal actions of thinking and feeling, planning and evaluating. The seven steps in this process are (1) becoming aware of negative feelings; (2) recognizing the need to change; (3) experiencing ambivalence; (4) reducing the risk through preparation; (5) letting it rest; (6) acting on the decision; and (7) evaluating the outcome.

STAGE 1: BECOMING AWARE OF NEGATIVE FEELINGS

We go along immersed in the flux of our lives, only occasionally stepping back or outside to look at ourselves, to question where we are going and what we're becoming. But unconsciously, often at the level of bodily sensations, we are giving ourselves messages all the time. Because these sensations are visceral, it's hard to put them into words. But each of us has some physical equivalent for "fear," for "despair," for "euphoria"—a dull pain in the gut, a feeling of heaviness inside, a perception that tears are close to welling up, a sense of soaring. Sometimes these feelings are hard to label, and sometimes they are hard to distinguish. Poets are usually better at describing these things. Emily Dickinson has tellingly characterized the feeling that accompanies loss:

> After great pain a formal feeling comes—
> The Nerves sit ceremonious, like Tombs*—

Most risky life changes are heralded in advance by just such physical cues. We may ignore them for a time, but eventually either they become too peremptory or they begin to translate themselves into verbal messages that can no longer be ignored: "I seem to feel lousy an awful lot of the time these days." "Something's wrong with my relationship with my wife. We never laugh any more." "I feel so burned out and trapped at work. I went into teaching full of idealism 15 years ago. And now all I think about is 3:30 and summer vacation."

We may project the blame outward: "No one understands me." "My wife's impossible to live with." "The bureaucrats and administrators take the joy out of teaching." But regardless of where we put the source of our discontent, in this initial phase most of us must sooner or later reckon with the feeling, "I don't like what I'm becoming." (These were the kinds of feelings described by

---

*From "After great pain," in *The Complete Poems of Emily Dickinson*, edited by Thomas H. Johnson (Boston: Little, Brown, 1960).

Celia, the pediatrician in Chapter 4, and Gary, the probation worker in Chapter 5.) The ultimate target of these negative feelings, whether conscious or unconscious, is the self. Once one has said "I feel trapped," "I feel stagnant," "I feel underused and unappreciated," the implied corollary is usually "And I don't want to be the kind of person who just lets this happen."

These feelings can persist for a short or long time, depending on one's ability to tolerate them, or one's masochism, or one's need for closure. We all know of stable but unhappy marriages that go on for decades, like George and Martha's in Edward Albee's *Who's Afraid of Virginia Woolf?* Conversely, some couples separate after the first major argument has destroyed their illusion of "happily ever after."

Whatever our flash points, at some time most of us will translate these feelings of dissatisfaction and loss of control into some more forward-looking project. At that point it's still much too early to speak of "plans." What we have, instead, is a sense of uneasiness and the feeling that something needs to be done about it.

STAGE 2: RECOGNIZING THE NEED TO CHANGE

The second stage is usually a subtle modulation from Stage 1, like a change of key from a minor to its corresponding major. Feelings of unease become translated at first into vague impulses: "I wish I could confront my father; maybe then I wouldn't feel so bad every time we see each other." "I wish I had the nerve to ask for a raise." "Boy, would I like to chuck this job and start on something entirely new."

These thoughts are wistful—full of yearning without much expectation of gratification—and yet they also contain a kernel of hope. The kernel often blooms in our fantasies, if we let it, into some happier idea of how we'd like things to be. The danger at this stage is that we will abort these fantasies as being distracting or unrealistic—merely wishful thinking. Dismissing these fantasies prematurely means ruling out possibilities. Early in any creative process—whether it is a literal act of creation or an act of self-*re*-creation, we must be charitable to our brainchildren. We must take the attitude of the good caretaker, who is cheerfully indulgent of the tiny infant while it is helpless and totally dependent. Our ideas and our fantasies need the same kind of care at their birth. If we neglect them, treat them with scorn, or impose premature strictures on them, they will shrivel and die, like the institutionalized children who die of wasting diseases because of insufficient loving attention.

Instead of dismissing them, we should learn to hail them and listen to them carefully, for they often embody our deepest needs. In fact, we can make a disciplined attempt to play out these fantasies and see where they lead.

In workshops on career change and on risk-taking, I have used a fantasy exercise to help people clarify what they would like to undertake but are afraid to try. Here is an example of one woman's responses (the exercise questions are in italics):

Fantasy Risk

Think of an important risk that you would like to take—something that is within your control but that you are afraid to initiate.

1. *Describe in some detail just what the risk is.* For once I would like to break away from the work ethic, the responsibility to work constantly 9–5, 250-odd days a year, and the security of a fixed income. My fantasy is that I will save about $4,000, take a leave of absence from work and exit, stage left, for Europe to explore, to travel, and to allow myself for 3–4 months the freedom to wake up each morning and proceed to do exactly what I want.

2. *What appeals to you about taking the risk? What would you gain from it—objectively and psychologically?* What's appealing? To focus again on what I would *like* to do rather than what I feel I *must* or *should* do. Psychologically, I believe the experience would allow me to be more open and would free me of my own sometimes rigid way of viewing life alternatives. Hopefully, I would learn that I could survive without that guaranteed biweekly check and those benefits for a time! Objectively, I would gain a wealth of knowledge, exposure to culture, art, and alternative styles of life. I would take the opportunity to become familiar with European vineyards and health systems. I would become more fluent in a language—probably French.

3. *What's frightening about the risk? What holds you back from taking it? What do you stand to lose?* Less and less is frightening. A year ago I would never have considered it. Now what holds me back, of course, is the capital. In a year, after saving, I will realize this. Then... what happens to the house while I'm gone? The cats? What if I can't speak the language? How will this 4-month "sabbatical" affect my work record? If my employer won't grant a 4-month leave of absence, will I leave anyway? I could stand to lose a job.

4. *What's the worst thing that could happen?* I'd lose my job, come back 4 months later, and be broke. I'd put off investing in a home.... I'd have nothing to show for the time.

5. *If the worst thing happened, then what could you do?* Look for and find another job.

6. *If you really wanted to pursue this risk, what's the first step? What's the second step?*
   a. Continue saving. Check with current employer about leave possibilities and alternatives. Begin now to expand my current skill to enhance my employability if I had to look for another job.
   b. Think of ways to relate the trip to my current field or areas of interest. In a job interview, then, I would be able to describe the employment lapse as an independent, self-initiated learning adventure.

This woman also wrote that she could start doing steps 6a and 6b right away and would have made substantial progress within a year, and that she could seal her commitment by telling her closest friend about her projected risk.

When we spell out our fantasies, we can use them to make the transition from "If only I could" to the determined "By God, I will"—I will approach my boss, I will start my own business, I will move to California, I will make my marriage work, I will learn to live alone, I will quit this research job I loathe, I *will*...

In this stage, fantasy must be given freedom to soar. It is only later in the process that we need—and can afford—to clip the wings of our fantasies, to domesticate them to our everyday world.

STAGE 3: EXPERIENCING AMBIVALENCE

The "I will" resolve, though reassuring, is likely to be unstable, particularly if the change we are contemplating is a big one. "I will" is almost always followed by "But can I?" as anxiety reasserts itself. This push toward the hoped-for future and the pull back to a known past are at the heart of the risk-taking process. It's no wonder that so many of my respondents described a mixture of emotions: afraid but excited, doubtful but hopeful, scared but determined.

What are we anxious about? We are anxious about losing something— losing our known world, whose predictability gives us control; losing our self-esteem if we fail; losing the love of others if we need to oppose or surpass them; and, of course, we may face tangible, material losses as well. A man who thinks about moving across country to look for a job faces the loss of his known place of residence, his enduring friends, his accustomed work. In any new job he may be trading the horrors he knows for those he can't yet imagine, and he is giving up a lot in the process.

When the Anxiety Is Too Great

If the prospect of undertaking a large change is so threatening that your stomach is constantly churning, you ruminate endlessly, you can't sleep, or you feel you're developing an ulcer, your body, in its wisdom, is telling you, "This is too big." Persisting in the face of transitory fear that is spiked with excitement is one thing. Persisting in the face of pervasive anxiety that floods out more positive feelings is another.

Christine, a highly skilled counselor in a university women's center, decided she needed to earn more money and, when approached by a prospective partner, she started an executive-recruitment agency. For weeks before making the move, she found that she was going home every night, getting into bed after dinner, and pulling the sheets over her head. She tried to make light of it by saying it was simply the terror anyone might feel at starting a major new venture. But Christine had taken many risks in her personal and professional life before ths one. Clearly, the physical response was evoked by something else. It was evoked, as she later discovered, by the deformation in her style that a hard-sell, aggressive recruiting enterprise would require. Her underlying fears turned out to be prophetic. The difference in styles between herself and her partner proved to be so handicapping to both of them that they disbanded the partnership after six months.

Mark, a young Ph.D. in sociology, was offered a job working with a professor who was doing research on the political socialization of children. Mark had written his dissertation on this subject at another university, so on paper this looked like the perfect first job for him—"tailor made," his thesis adviser told him. But Mark knew that the project director had the reputation of being a difficult, contentious man, who was good to his staff only so long as they were deferential and dependent. Mark worried about how his own need for autonomy could be met in this situation, but he put this worry aside, on the ground that the work so neatly dovetailed with his dissertation research: Shortly before taking the job, he developed a peptic ulcer. He worked on the project for two years but found it a difficult assignment that ultimately impaired his self-esteem and his efficiency. The ulcer was a warning signal he had ignored at his own peril.

The moral seems clear: In planning a change, if your body is telling you "stop," and if the pluses are experienced only abstractly and "on paper," the risk should be refused. Refusing may also represent a risk—the risk of trusting your deep feelings more than some abstract notion of what ought to be best for you. This feels particularly dangerous for anxious (Style A) risk takers (like Alan, the computer analyst described in Chapter 3). Considerations of this sort make it clear that although lists or inventories may be useful guides in making risky decisions, they ultimately cannot work unless there is some provision for psychologically weighting the items. One ulcer pang may counterbalance a host of theoretical pluses. Style A decision makers, especially, may need to learn to take into account these nonverbal, nonrational cues about projected decisions.

When the Anxiety Is Minimal

What if you experience very little anxiety at an impending risk, very few negative feelings? Three circumstances could account for this lack of ambivalence:

1. This is not really a risk. If what you are moving toward has many virtues and a highly predictable outcome, there is almost no danger involved.
2. The negative aspects of the existing situation are so overwhelming that it seems that no choice is involved. If *everything* about your present job is unbearable, for example—the duties, the pace, the co-workers, the boss—then the decision to change feels not like a decision but like a compulsion. In such cases, we commonly say, as Jules and Gary (in

Chapter 5) did, "I had no choice." Without a sense of choice, there is little feeling of ambivalence.

3. You are avoiding, rationalizing, or denying the anxiety you actually do feel.

The last category is of greatest interest here. My own research data have shown that the very few people who reported negative outcomes either had prepared inadequately or had felt "blindly optimistic" at the outset— *overwhelmingly* hopeful and excited, with no sense of possible loss. *Inner, emotional preparation*—which takes account of losses as well as gains, fears as well as hopes—is as necessary a prerequisite for successful risk taking as any of the other preparatory steps I will outline in Stage 4.

Looked at slightly differently, anxiety is an appropriate response, because in contemplating any major change, we are giving up valued connections. Such mourning is as necessary in confronting the potential losses of risk taking as in dealing with the actual losses of death and separation. No one can say for certain whether it is better to mourn in advance of or following a loss; this is partly a matter of style. But it may be that the mourning that finally catches up with us in the face of earlier denial is more virulent for having been suppressed. Thus, after reading the section on himself in this book, Jules told me that he was struck by how much he had denied the losses involved in leaving New York to come to California and that they finally hit him with a wallop. People who are Style C risk takers—those who are impulsive or who deny real dangers—have trouble mourning in anticipation. They often feel that acknowledging pain inhibits them from acting. If they can learn to anticipate problems *even a little*, they may be able to experience an attenuated form of the negative feeling that will hit eventually—rather like the vaccine that uses the attenuated form of a virus as a preventive against the actual disease.

We know from the abundant literature that "griefwork" is an essential part of the healing process in confronting the death or loss of someone we love. One of the most moving accounts of such a loss is *A Grief Observed*, a slim volume by English philosopher-essayist C. S. Lewis, who described in journal form the mourning that followed the death of his dearly beloved wife, whom he calls H. Lewis begins: "No one ever told me that grief is so like fear. I am not afraid, but the sensation is like being afraid. The same fluttering in the stomach, the same restlessness, the yawning. I keep on swallowing." Sometime later in his mourning, he writes that grief still feels like fear or, perhaps, more like suspense: "I think I am beginning to understand why grief feels like suspense. It comes from the frustration of so many impulses that had become habitual. Thought after thought, feeling after feeling, action after action, had H. for their object. Now their target is gone." He is thus left with a constant sense of unpredictability as well as emptiness.

This kind of griefwork is not just a passive suffering, according to many writers—beginning, notably, with Sigmund Freud in "Mourning and Melancholia"—but is an active process of disengaging from the loved person bit by bit, in context after context. We know that those who do not mourn sufficiently— that is, mourn long and intensely enough—are highly susceptible to psychosomatic or psychological disorders months and even years later. I am certainly not suggesting that we enter into deep mourning every time we contemplate a risk; that would indeed be counterproductive and paralyzing. I *am* suggesting that some of our fear in changing is a kind of mourning and that we may need to pay explicit homage to what we're giving up: the choices we had to foreclose, the alternate roads not taken, the friends we're leaving behind, the pleasures of singlehood, the familiarity of places, the comforting security of even a job we can no longer stand.

All these things—what we stand to lose presently and in the future—may keep our resolve to change somewhat unstable. C. S. Lewis writes: "In grief nothing stays put: One keeps on emerging from a phase, but it always recurs. Round and round. Everything repeats." If we substitute *fear* for *grief,* we can see how this feeling applies in risk taking, for any large change means giving up something that is known and predictable, however painful. It means facing what we cannot anticipate. Therefore, except in those rare instances when we feel "I had no choice," it is only natural that, having determined resolutely to alter the course of our life, we should toss back and forth between fear and hope, exhilaration and anxiety, panic and a sense of high adventure. Some people can't tolerate such conflicting feelings; they rationalize away the need for change, saying, "Well, things aren't that bad" or "Maybe next year."

For the same reasons, many people would like to short-circuit this process, to proceed easily and directly from the wish for change to the action that sets change in motion. But mixed feelings *need* to surface. Some may say, "This exciting change that I'm looking forward to can't be right for me if I feel really scared." Perhaps they should say, rather, that the risk can't be right if they *don't* feel scared—at least a little.

At bottom, we are talking about degrees of anxiety—what is optimal, how much is too much. Anxiety that is about to make you ill, that becomes obsessive and invades your dreams, is obviously too much anxiety. But the transitory heart-knocking, boot-quaking anxiety that is also associated with a shiver of anticipation may be the signal that you're into something big.

The ultimate question is whether you can use the anxiety. Can you manage it? We know from the large experimental literature on human and animal learning that a certain amount of anxiety (drive level, motivation, arousal) is necessary to get us moving. In a satiated, totally unmotivated organism, nothing much happens. Conversely, too much anxiety may cause flight or freezing. The issue, again, is not *whether* a person is afraid but *how* afraid, and what he or she has been motivated to learn to do in the fear-producing situation. As we saw in Chapter 7, rats can learn coping responses while afraid, fighter pilots can perform more efficiently under mild fear, and performers can learn to harness their fear of exposure. Performing *while afraid* is what enhances our sense of mastery.

In summary, then, experiencing ambivalence means experiencing, simultaneously or in close succession, desires to approach and desires to avoid, pushes and pulls. One day you think, "Of course I can change fields. Lots of people do it. It can't be so difficult." The next day—or perhaps even the next moment—you think, "No, it's just too damned hard; there are too many unknowns. I'm better off staying put." And the pushes and pulls go on. In undertaking a risk, we really need both kinds of feelings. The anticipation of gains keeps us going forward, while anxiety about losses keeps us from going too fast or too recklessly. Careless (Style C) risk takers need to search for the difficulties and tolerate some anxiety; anxious (Style A) risk takers need to look for the pluses. Each of these types tends to focus one-sidedly on possible outcomes. When we are taking a big step, experiencing ambivalence not only is sensible, it is *necessary* to keep the risk taking in balance. *When fear is balanced by a sense of excitement and purpose, it offers an emotional preparation for the risk we are undertaking.*

It may be reassuring to know that the preaction phases of any risk taking are generally the most frightening. As one of my research subjects aptly put it: "Just deciding to take the risk is the most risky thing most of the time." This point of view is corroborated by predecision research, including an interesting study in which sport parachute jumpers were asked, retrospectively, to rate their anxiety at different points during a Sunday on which they were jumping. Was their anxiety highest as they boarded the plane? Was it highest as they were about to hurl themselves out into space? Most people imagine that the instant before jumping would be the most frightening moment. In fact, however, these jumpers reported feeling the greatest fear when they were *still on the ground,* making the decision whether or not to sign up for the jump that day. In other words, once in action, you generally will find the situation less fearful than it was when you were initially contemplating the possibilities or deciding on a choice. But—and it's a big but—that reduction in anxiety is hollow *unless you have adequately prepared for the action.* The various means of preparation—all of which are, in fact, attempts to circumscribe or reduce the risk—comprise the next necessary phase.

STAGE 4: REDUCING THE RISK THROUGH PREPARATION

Drawing on analogies from biology, we again turn to Jonathan Miller's *The Body in Question.* In comparing the defenses of various species, Miller writes: "The most versatile and ambitious species are those which have evolved mechanisms capable of recognizing and facing threats before they have had a chance to inflict expensive and possibly irreparable damage." Miller makes the point that species that have an assortment of protective mechanisms are much better off than those that depend on only one kind of permanent protection—such as the turtle, most of whose energy is spent in "moving its safety from one place to the next." Agility and resourcefulness give the higher mammals the possibility of adapting to many more circumstances.

Taking our cue from this principle, then, what kind of resourcefulness can we introduce in preparing for risk? We have already talked about the emotional preparation of experiencing—and welcoming—ambivalence, but what about other kinds of preparation that in effect constitute ways to reduce the risk?

A Misconception: Is It "Cheating" to Reduce the Risk?"

It always surprises me to learn that many people think of taking a risk as doing something in which the odds are formidably stacked against them—playing Russian roulette, diving into 3 feet of water from a 30-foot diving board, performing Evel Knievel feats across chasms—the acts of physical derring-do we associate with stunt people and adventurers. They thus fail to give themselves credit for the smaller but still demanding chances they themselves take.

A woman teacher says, for example, "I'm okay at taking risks only if I can psych myself into believing there is an exit. I don't usually use it, but thinking of risks as permanent tends to paralyze me." You can hear the apologetic tone of her statement.

Similarly, a school counselor says, "It is hard for me to really take a risk, knowing I may see defeat. I only accept risks that are attainable ones." Again, he sounds a note of self-criticism and seems to imply that one really ought to undertake risks that are *un*attainable.

A middle-aged journalist writes:

> I'm not a risk taker; I like to have bases covered, plans of action thought out before I make moves. Even in risky situations I manage to have "cushions" built in. One example is what happened when I left my first husband. I was terrified since my family didn't approve. However, looking back at the situation, I had much support, friends helping, the financial situation thought out, etc. So in some sense it wasn't a risk.

Such responses suggest that people sometimes castigate themselves for reducing the danger in risky situations, as though the only way one could earn credit for taking chances would be to do so impulsively, blindly, and without preparation. This perception is counterproductive and leads people to give themselves inaccurate messages both about the nature of the world and about themselves. Instead of thinking, "I'm someone who is rightly aware of how hard it is to make major changes, so I do whatever I can to make it easier for myself and therefore more likely that I will move ahead," they tell themselves, "I am really timid. The only risks that count are those that stack the odds against you. It's 'cheating' to use a safety net when you walk the high wire." Far from cheating, reducing the risk is essential. We know from decision theory that the worst decisions are made under the following conditions:

1. The decision is a "hot" or major one.
2. The consequences of the person's action are largely unknown.
3. The decision must be made quickly.
4. The decision is likely to be irreversible.
5. Because of the other four conditions (the significance, uncertainty, urgency, and irreversibility of the decision), the person is highly anxious.

It follows that to make good decisions, we must control the elements of the risk that are controllable. Since we are dealing here with major life decisions, we cannot easily control the first of the conditions above, although, as will become evident, we can reduce the scale by reframing the problem. But what about the rest—can we reduce the uncertainty, reduce the urgency, reduce the irreversibility? Is there anything else we can do to reduce the anxiety? Let's look at these possibilities as we attempt to shift the balance of ambivalence, making it easier to move ahead.

Reducing the Urgency

Some people function well under tight deadlines; these are often the procrastinators, who feel that they do their best work only when they have to produce while racing against the clock. The urgency overcomes their resistance. But other people panic when they have to do work or to make decisions under acute time pressure. What can such people do? They can move up the deadline insofar as that is possible. People often have a sense that a time limit— particularly one imposed by someone else—is sacrosanct; on closer examination, however, it may well turn out to be more elastic. A prospective employer will wait another day or two while you mull over a job decision. A publisher will extend the deadline for something you're writing. Remember that Jenny and Bob Mitchell gave themselves more time in their decision about having a child by investigating the latest medical research, which showed that the relatively safe childbearing deadline was later than they had thought at first.

Getting others to extend a deadline is one thing; allowing *yourself* to extend a deadline is another. I am struck in my therapeutic work by how often a sense of urgency is misplaced. Style A people—the anxious risk takers like Alan—typically give themselves deadlines that are often quite arbitrary, being set more by their internal harsh taskmasters than by what's reasonable or required by others. Much of what I do as a therapist is to help people give themselves time to reflect and understand what's happening, to show them which part of the urgency is of their own making.

Marjorie, a woman I saw in therapy, told me of a fight she had had with her husband two nights earlier. A usually highly controlled man, Leonard had exploded: their marriage wasn't working, her job took her away too much, they didn't have enough time together, and he was fed up. Marjorie was so panicked that the next day she was on the verge of chucking her job and looking immediately for a less demanding one that involved less commuting. But when she returned home that night, her husband had cooled off, and he admitted he had overreacted the night before. If she had been catapulted into action by her sense of urgency, she might have made a short-sighted and disastrous move.

A false sense of urgency may arise in people who are naturally fearful and used to complying or in people who cannot stand being in a state of indecision. But if you can learn to allow yourself breathing or incubating time in any major life decision, you may well find that what was labored and sweated over, vigorously sought and pursued, will come to you in a mysterious, almost effortless way. I will have more to say about this in the discussion of Stage 5: Letting It Rest.

Reducing the Uncertainty: Information Seeking and Rehearsal

Seeking information is probably the most basic step in illuminating the dark, unknown world we are entering when we initiate radical change. Although the Wheelis quotation at the beginning of this chapter emphasizes that the course and result of such change is ultimately unknowable, there are guides or maps for at least parts of this journey.

In contemplating a change of careers, for example, we need two kinds of information—knowledge about ourselves (our skills, talents, abilities, fantasies, and aspirations) and knowledge about "what's out there"—the labor market. What are the expanding fields? What are the shrinking ones? What's the realistic chance of being able to make it in real estate after having been a teacher for ten years—given your temperament and the money supply? Computer programming is an expanding field; could you do that kind of work if you have a horror of math? (Answer: You very well might, since computer programming correlates more highly with language skills than with mathematics skills.) What books can you read? Whom can you talk to in the field you may be interested in? What kind of professional guidance—through workshops or individual counseling—can round out what you learn on your own? What tests can you take that will help you become more aware of your skills and interests and transferable accomplishments? How can you convert those free-form fantasies you have had into well-shaped plans?

The mechanics of career change have been thoroughly described in a number of books (some of them already referred to in the section on Yvonne's career change and listed in the bibliography). The basic strategy behind all of them is to increase your self-knowledge and your knowledge about careers so that, by reducing ignorance and eliminating irrelevant information, you can make a better match between yourself and work.

Another means for reducing uncertainty is to use techniques of practicing, rehearsing, or sampling what you're getting into. It includes spending time with the infant of friends if you've never been around a young baby and are thinking of having a child. It includes role-playing a job interview before actually going on one, or getting permission to "shadow" someone who is doing the kind of work you think you want; after spending a day at his or her side, you will have a clearer moment-by-moment feel of what the work is like. It includes living with someone before committing yourself to marriage, or separating for a short time as a prelude to possible divorce. It includes taking a job on probation to see how you and it work together. It includes taking an internship as an introduction to a field. It includes launching an interest you will pursue in retirement long before you actually retire.

The rehearsing techniques will help you map the terrain; the trial arrangements will also do that and will give you an opportunity to reverse gears if you find you have made a mistake. (I will discuss this further in the section "Reducing the Irreversibility.")

These techniques not only will reduce uncertainty by providing information, but they will also serve to temper your fantasies, which, although they are valuable spurs, are also often idealized. Now is the time to scale down the dreams you freely elaborated earlier. These information-seeking and rehearsing procedures will reduce uncertainty and misconceptions and thereby lessen anxiety. But lowering anxiety depends on more than cognitive activities. It also depends on human reassurance.

Reducing the Anxiety by Seeking Support

Dispelling misinformation and reducing ignorance make us feel more secure. But we don't live by facts alone. When we undertake a large new venture, we need to feel that people care, that they are standing by with encouragement and sometimes with guidance. This support can come from a mate, a family, friends, people in similar situations, and in some cases from a spiritual advisor or professional counselor. This support-seeking process can contribute to our sense of mastery because our feelings are shared and given names and because we realize that others have had similar experiences. (Again and again, the experience of people in therapy groups or support groups is, "I thought I was the only one who had those feelings. I had no idea that almost everyone feels the way I do.")

The balance between information seeking and support seeking may vary from risk to risk. In a divorce, for example, although information about legal and financial arrangements may be important, emotional support may in fact be more necessary. In other kinds of risks (e.g., change of careers) information may be more crucial than emotional support. Ultimately, every risk requires some of both.

Reducing the Irreversibility: Keeping Bridges Unburned, Laying Down Safety Nets

We know that one reason major life changes evoke so much anxiety is that they appear to be irreversible. But just as the urgency of making a risky decision is sometimes misperceived, so, too, is the irreversibility of the choice assumed without being sufficiently tested. If we think hard and creatively enough, this irreversibility often turns out to be less stringent than we had believed. Some decisions *are* virtually irreversible, such as deciding to have a child; for most people, giving up a child would be unthinkable. For many other decisions, however, we can build in fail-safe and retreat positions—"just in case." Thus, taking a leave rather than quitting, even from a job you really don't want to go back to, may help reduce your anxiety and fantasies of the almshouse, so that (particularly if you are a worrisome, Style A person) you'll be better equipped to tackle the challenge of traveling abroad or setting up your own business.

Even if you can't go home again, you can have a contingency plan for an alternative course of action if the present one turns out to be a disaster. Just knowing that there are other possibilities, that you don't have only one choice, reduces the risk. That is why the fantasy risk exercise asked: "What's the worst thing that could happen, and what could you do if it did happen?" Most people find it very relieving to look at the worst possible outcome and see that they would have some way to deal with it.

Reducing the Scale of the Risk by Restructuring It

This operation, which consists of reducing the risk by redefining or relabeling it or by breaking it into its component parts, takes place largely inside our heads. As Epictetus said, "It is not the things themselves which trouble us, but the opinion we have about these things." In their book *Change*, Paul Watzlawick and his coauthors speak of the work they do to "reframe" situations as therapists dealing with family systems:

> To reframe...means to change the conceptual and/or emotional setting or viewpoint in relation to which a situation is experienced and to place it in another frame which fits the "facts" of the same concrete situation equally well or even better, and thereby changes its entire meaning.

We can change the emotional setting of a task or risk by giving it a different value or priority in our lives. One form of restructuring is to look at the other side—a task of which I'm always aware in therapeutic work. This requires asking "What am I leaving out?" "What are the pluses, if I'm focusing only on the negatives?" or, conversely, "What are the losses, if I'm focusing only on the gains?" The thrust of this entire book has been to look at both sides of moving on and staying in place. Having a balanced view reduces the actual risk by showing us a large segment of reality, instead of a narrow slice.

Another way to restructure is to change the priority that we are giving a certain risk, to ask, "If I fail at this does it mean I'm a total failure? Are there other things in life that are at least as important to me? If I do poorly at my job, does that have to define me, or can I invest more interest in being a friend or a father, or some other role?"

Speaking of failure reminds us that we can also change the frame or context in which we put a situation. As we saw in the previous chapter, we can shift the frame from success versus failure to learning versus not learning. In this way, we have changed the pattern. We can almost always learn from our failures, but we do *not* always learn from our successes.

Finally, we can change our strategy or focus. Instead of perceiving a risk as huge and undifferentiated, we can break it down into its components. So long as we perceive it the first way, it will seem overwhelming. When we relabel it or break it down into components, smaller parts begin to take on shape, to make sense, and therefore to become manageable. It's like the process by which we discriminate the Big Dipper among a blur of stars on a clear night, with the feeling, "There's something I recognize!" How we circumscribe the flux in a life change can vary tremendously. People I have talked to about major life change, such as divorce, often have reiterated some version of a theme: "I could do it by taking just one day at a time," or "If I thought of the next step and just concentrated on that, it was a lot easier than envisioning the whole thing." In this kind of scaling-down process, the formidable and shapeless challenge "I've got to change careers" becomes the feasible "Tomorrow I have to go on an information interview."

The tendency to defeat oneself by making global responses can be seen especially clearly in people with depressive tendencies. It often turns out that the underlying belief of those who are feeling helpless and hopeless is, "If I can't do any one thing, I can't do everything," or, conversely, "If I can't do everything, I can't do anything." These false generalizations stem from perfectionist notions, and they increase feelings of ineffectiveness.

What we should be telling ourselves instead is, "Here is this big, messy challenge. Let's see if I can give it some form by breaking it into parts. That's the first step. And when I've done that, let's see what is the smallest part I can handle effectively right now." Keeping our eyes fixed too far ahead causes us to stumble.

An example may make this clearer:

Michael, a graduate student in comparative literature, was blocked about his dissertation, which was to be a critical analysis of *Don Quixote*. He kept going around and around with "When I write my dissertation," "If I write my dissertation," "When I finish the dissertation," although he had not even started it after six years in graduate school.

Part of the problem was his globalizing. As Michael realized this, he was encouraged to begin in the least presumptuous and committing way. He was helped to start thinking of what he was doing *not* as writing a dissertation, but simply as jotting down ideas. He was to write in pencil on a yellow-lined pad, in order to indicate to himself that the procedure was tentative, loose, and unbinding. Pencil was less permanent, less forbidding than typewriter or even pen and ink.

In addition to changing the mechanics, Michael learned to use a strategy that was both improvisatory and facilitating. At first, he wrote only when an idea "seized him," rather than tracking it futilely through thickets of resistance. He thus developed skill at being receptive to whatever welled up inside him spontaneously. He told himself that he was merely writing "chunks" or "fragments"—whatever came into his head, without relation to an overall grand design—on the grounds that, when he had accumulated enough of these fragments, they would coalesce in his mind, and the order would flow from them rather than being imposed *on* them. Working in this way, Michael was able to produce an original and important dissertation in a relatively short time.

Michael's ability to tolerate temporarily a lack of structure was, in effect, a vote of confidence for his preconscious mental processes. Such relaxation permits unanticipated ideas to develop and allows "notions," which are less fixed and more quirky than ideas, to flourish. Respect for these preconscious processes is also required in the next stage of the risk-taking process.

STAGE 5: LETTING IT REST—INCUBATING THE FINAL MOVE

After rationally reducing the risk in any way we can, as suggested in Stage 4, the next step is to "let go" of the process, to let it "sit" or incubate—even if only briefly. This letting go may have to occur more than once in a risk-taking process, as we turn away from our objective and let some deeper part of ourselves—our preconscious or unconscious—have its say. We have all had the experience at one time or another of having a solution that we had labored or sweated over come to us suddenly and without effort. Probably the most common experience of this sort is groping futilely for a name or a memory, which, soon after we give up pursuing it, will obligingly swim up to the surface of our consciousness.

Such incubation is certainly necessary for creative work, in which trying to force a product will only generate more panic and more resistance. It is also true in any creative self-defining experience, and that is what risk taking ultimately is. Every major decision is an act of self-creation and calls on many of the same skills as creative work in general.

Turning away or letting go may look like procrastination, but it can be distinguished on two grounds. First, we consent to it, rather than feeling guilty about it. Second, it represents not a shutting down but rather an attentive waiting, a poised readiness. And, as Shakespeare has taught us, "The readiness is all." Sometimes we move ahead by sitting still for awhile. Learning theorists have established that performance in a task often improves after an interruption. Some fallow time seems necessary if the seeds of our risk are to germinate and sprout. At some point—particularly before moving into action—it is not only permissible but desirable to let go, so that our deepest convictions can emerge.

STAGE 6: TAKING THE PLUNGE—ACTING ON THE DECISION

If your cognitive and emotional preparation is sound, if you have done whatever you can to make the risk manageable and to protect against disaster, and if you have let the decision settle till it feels right, you are ready to move into action. No matter how elaborate the preparation, this stage always demands a leap into the unknown in some ways. In addition to what is unknown in the situation, you always face something unknown in yourself. As John Fowles wrote: "At some point in all the major decisions of life...reason and intelligence and scholarship become powerless to help; so one must either live in perpetual doubt and anguish or step into the dark." Whether we speak of groping or stepping or leaping or plunging, our images all convey a spurt of forward movement into an unknown element. Even people who have deliberated and mulled over their risky decisions usually experience the actual moment of putting them into effect as "taking the plunge." All our rational planning leads, if only for a moment, to an act of faith.

This moment may disorient us, as all moments of free fall disrupt our sense of time and place. But it also may feel like the least risky step in the process, for it usually brings a heady sense of release: "I've done this dreaming and thinking and worrying and planning, and now at last I'm ready to quit my job" (or take a lover, or get married, or get on the boat alone, or accept the higher-level job, or conceive a child...). Remember the study that showed that Sunday skydivers felt less afraid when they actually were about to hurl themselves into space than when they were on the ground making their decision whether or not to jump that day.

STAGE 7: EVALUATING THE OUTCOME

Many people—perhaps most of us—are used to thinking that taking action is the end of the risk-taking process, but it really isn't. Apart from the continuing risks one takes after the launch, there is a final phase that requires us to step back and to sum up.

This evaluation, like most of the processes I have talked about, has two aspects—outer and inner. You need to evaluate the "reality" outcome of the risk you have taken. Was confronting your father worth the anxiety it generated—did it improve relations between the two of you? Did accepting the teaching job in a ghetto school work out—did the children learn more and make you feel it was worth the effort? Did the vacation home you went into hock to buy turn out to be a costly mistake or a much-used hideaway that justified the sacrifice? These are "reality" questions—questions about how things worked out practically both for you and for the others who were implicated in your risk.

In addition, every risk has an internal component: how you feel about yourself as a consequence of taking the risk. This, too, should be examined. Having won or lost—how do you feel about having taken the chance? The two kinds of outcomes often go together. *But as we have seen repeatedly, they don't have to.* I am struck by how often people will say things such as the following—in this case, a statement by a woman who chose to come with her husband from Europe to America to take a new job in a strange land, without friends or family:

> I feel good that I took the plunge. Proud of myself for going through the hardship and growing tremendously through it. Yet I do not feel quite "there" yet, since I'm trapped into teaching again and experience some of the same fear of the unknown. But at least this time I feel stronger. I know it's not a job that I'm looking for, it's my own self, which means that my whole life is at stake and in my hands.

People have told me again and again that even when things didn't work out as they'd hoped, they were nevertheless pleased with themselves for venturing, for asserting themselves, for testing their mettle, for *not* stagnating. If you choose to take on a big challenge and really give it your all by going through each stage of the process fully, you are bound to experience yourself as more purposive and more courageous. Then, the next time you approach another challenge, you will feel like—and be—a more effective risk taker.

I think of the problem posed by risk taking as the existential choice between two difficult alternatives. It is the choice Odysseus made on his long sea voyage home, when, in navigating the Straits of Messina, he had to steer between Scylla and Charybdis—between the six-headed monster that could devour a sailor with each of its mouths and the fearsome whirlpool that sucked ships into its swirling depths. When Odysseus asked Circe, the sorceress, for advice on how to chart this tricky course, she counseled Odysseus to steer closer to Scylla, the dragon, rather than risk Charybdis, the whirlpool.

About this choice, psychiatrist Wolfgang Lederer wrote:

> Circe was right, for the Scylla, that many-toothed, many-headed monster, is a perfect allegory for anxiety and fear. And Charybdis, with its downward sweep into darkness...an image of depression; and the sea-voyage, finally, an excellent symbol for life itself.... And what the image conveys to us is this: that if we withdraw from what is frightening...then we fall into depression, a stage

experienced as dark and downward, utterly without hope or exit, leading only to death. Whereas if we wish to emerge from depression, we have to face anxiety once again—a frightening prospect, but one offering a chance at the future, a chance of survival and success.*

In moving away from the Charybdis of despair, the more we understand and prepare for our risks, the easier it will be to outwit the Scylla of our anxiety, to know that we have overcome.

*From Wolfgang Lederer, "How Does One Cure a Soul?" *The College* (a publication of St. John's College, Annapolis, Md.) 28 (April 1976):1–11.

Self-Assessment Exercise 3: Fantasy Risk

Rather than ending with a neat summary, this book ends with a chance to apply what you have learned by allowing yourself to envision and begin to plan for your next risk. On a large pad or an 8½″ × 11″ sheet of paper, write your answers to the following questions.

Think of an important risk that you would like to take soon—something that is within your control but that you are afraid to initiate.

1. Describe in some detail what the risk is.
2. What appeals to you about taking this risk? What would you gain from it—objectively and psychologically?
3. What's frightening about the risk? What holds you back from taking it, and what do you stand to lose?
4. What's the worst thing that could happen if you took the chance and it turned out badly?
5. If the worst thing happened, then what could you do?
6. If you need information to pursue this risk, where could you go for it?
7. From whom could you get support?
8. What could you do to make this risk less risky? What kinds of measures could you build in to make it
   a. less urgent?
   b. less irreversible?
   c. less overwhelming?
9. What aspect of your own style of making risky decisions (the ones you learned about in Exercise 1) do you need to allow or correct for in taking this risk?
10. Suppose you were to break this risk into small steps:
    a. What would the first step be? How soon could you take it?
    b. What would the second step be? How soon could you take it?
11. Sometimes you can help commit yourself to a course of action if you tell someone about your plan. What person can you tell about this fantasy to make it more real?

Bibliography

Abelson, R. P. "Computer Simulation of 'Hot' Cognition." In *Computer Simulation of Personality,* ed. S. Tomkins and S. Messick. New York: Wiley, 1963.

Ainsworth, M. D. S.; Blehar, M.; Waters, E.; and Wall, S. *Patterns of Attachment.* Hillsdale, N.J.: Erlbaum, 1978.

Alloy, L. B., and Abramson, L. W. "Judgment of Contingency in Depressed and Nondepressed Students: Sadder but Wiser." *Journal of Experimental Psychology: General* 108(1979):441–485.

American Psychiatric Association. *Diagnostic and Statistical Manual of Mental Disorders,* 3rd ed. Washington, D.C.: American Psychiatric Association, Committee on Nomenclature and Statistics, 1980.

American Psychiatric Association. *Quick Reference to the Diagnostic Criteria from DSM-III* (Mini-D). Washington, D.C.: American Psychiatric Association, 1980.

Atkinson, J. W. "Motivational Determinants of Risk-taking Behavior." *Psychological Review* 64(1957):359–372.

Atkinson, J. W., ed. *Motives in Fantasy, Action, and Society.* Princeton: Van Nostrand, 1964.

Atkinson, J. W., and Feather, N. T., eds. *A Theory of Achievement Motivation.* New York: Wiley, 1966.

Atkinson, J. W., and Litwin, G. H. "Achievement Motive and Test Anxiety Conceived as Motive to Approach Success and Motive to Avoid Failure." *Journal of Abnormal and Social Psychology* 60(1960):52–63.

Auden, W. H. *Collected Poems*, ed. Edward Mendelson. New York: Random House, 1976.

Beck, A. T. *Depression: Causes and Treatment*. Philadelphia: University of Pennsylvania Press, 1970.

Bellow, Saul. *Henderson the Rain King*. New York: Viking, 1959.

Bloch, Chana. "Fear of Falling." Baccalaureate address, Mills College, Oakland, California, May 29, 1976.

Bolles, Richard. *What Color Is Your Parachute?: A Practical Manual for Job-Hunters and Career Changers*, rev. ed. Berkeley: Ten Speed Press, 1972.

Brumbaugh, R. S. *The Philosophers of Greece*. New York: Crowell, 1964.

Burnstein, E. "Fear of Failure, Achievement Motivation, and Aspiring to Prestigeful Occupations." *Journal of Abnormal and Social Psychology* 67(1963):189–193.

Butler, Samuel. *The Way of All Flesh*. New York: Dutton, 1913.

Cannon, W. B. *The Wisdom of the Body*. New York: Norton, 1939.

Coopersmith, Stanley. *The Antecedents of Self-esteem*. San Francisco: Freeman, 1967.

Corson, S. A., and Corson, E. O'L. "Constitutional Difference in Physiological Adaptation to Stress and Distress." In *Psychopathology of Human Adaptation*, ed. George Serban. New York: Plenum Press, 1976.

Dember, W. N. *The Psychology of Perception*. New York: Holt, 1960.

Dickinson, Emily. *The Complete Poems of Emily Dickinson*, ed. T. H. Johnson. Boston: Little, Brown, 1960.

Diener, C. I., and Dweck, C. S. "An Analysis of Learned Helplessness: II. The Processing of Success." *Journal of Personality and Social Psychology* 39(1980):940–952.

Dodge, D. L., and Martin, W. T. *Social Stress and Chronic Illness: Mortality Patterns in Industrial Society*. Notre Dame: Notre Dame University Press, 1970.

Dohrenwend, B. S., and Dohrenwend, B. P., eds. *Stressful Life Events: Their Nature and Effects*. New York: Wiley, 1974.

Erikson, E. H. *Childhood and Society*, 2nd ed. New York: Norton, 1963.

Erikson, E. H. *Identity, Youth and Crisis*. New York: Norton, 1968.

Fenichel, Otto. "The Counter-Phobic Attitude." *International Journal of Psychoanalysis* 20(1939):263–274.

Flavell, J. H. *The Developmental Psychology of Jean Piaget*. Princeton: Van Nostrand, 1963.

Fowles, John. *The Aristos*. New York: New American Library, 1975.

Freud, Sigmund. "Mourning and Melancholia" (1917). In *Collected Papers*, vol. 4. New York: Basic Books, 1959.

Freud, Sigmund. "Some Character Types Met With in Psychoanalytic Work" (1915). In *Collected Papers*, vol. 4. New York: Basic books, 1959.

Fuller, J. L. "Experimental Deprivation and Later Behavior." *Science* 158(29 December 1967):1645–1653.

Hartmann, Heinz. *Ego Psychology and the Problem of Adaptation*. New York: International Universities Press, 1939 (reprinted 1958).

Hoffer, Eric. *The Ordeal of Change*. New York: Harper, 1952.

Holmes, T. H., and Masuda, Minoru. "Life Change and Illness Susceptibility." In

Stressful Life Events: Their Nature and Effects, ed. B. S. Dohrenwend and B. P. Dohrenwend. New York: Wiley, 1974.

Horner, M. S. "Fail: Bright Women." *Psychology Today* 62(November 1969):36–38.

Horner, M. S. "The Measurement and Behavioral Implications of Fear of Success in Women." In *Motivation and Achievement,* ed. J. W. Atkinson and J. O. Raynor. New York: Wiley, 1974.

Horner, M. S., and Walsh, M. K. "Psychological Barriers to Success in Women." In *Women and Success,* ed. Ruth Kundsin. New York: Morrow, 1974.

Irish, R. K. *If Things Don't Improve Soon, I'm Going to Ask You to Fire Me: The Management Book for Everyone Who Works.* New York: Doubleday, 1975.

Janis, I. L., and Mann, Leon. *Decision Making: A Psychological Analysis of Conflict, Choice and Commitment.* New York: Free Press, 1977.

Kobasa, S. C.; Maddi, S. R.; and Kahn, Stephen. "Hardiness and Health: A Prospective Study." *Journal of Personality and Social Psychology* 42(1982):168–177.

Kogan, Nathan, and Dorros, Karen. "Sex Differences in Risk Taking and Its Attribution." *Sex Roles* 4(1978):755–765.

Kogan, Nathan, and Wallach, M. A. *Risk-Taking: A Study in Cognition and Personality.* New York: Holt, Rinehart & Winston, 1964.

Kogan, Nathan, and Wallach, M. A. "Risk-taking as a Function of the Situation, the Person and the Group." In *New Directions in Psychology III,* ed. George Mandler and Paul Mussen. New York: Holt, Rinehart & Winston, 1967.

Laing, R. D. *The Divided Self.* New York: Pantheon, 1960.

Lederer, Wolfgang. "How Does One Cure a Soul?" *The College* (a publication of St. John's College, Annapolis, Md.) 28(April 1976):1–11.

Levinson, Daniel. *The Seasons of a Man's Life.* New York: Knopf, 1978.

Lewis, C. S. *A Grief Observed.* Greenwich, Conn.: Seabury Press, 1963.

Loeb, Armin; Beck, A. T.; Diggory, J. C.; and Tuthill, Robert. "Expectancy, Level of Aspiration, Performance, and Self-Evaluation and Depression." Paper presented at the Annual Convention of the American Psychological Association, 1967.

Maccoby, E. E., and Jacklin, C. N. *The Psychology of Sex Differences.* Stanford: Stanford University Press, 1974.

Mahone, C. H. "Fear of Failure and Unrealistic Vocational Aspiration." *Journal of Abnormal and Social Psychology* 60(1960):253–261.

Marris, Peter. *Loss and Change.* New York: Anchor Books, 1975.

Maugham, W. S. *Creatures of Circumstance.* Garden City, N.Y.: Doubleday, 1947.

May, Robert. *Sex and Fantasy: Patterns of Male and Female Development.* New York: Norton, 1980.

Miller, Jonathan. *The Body in Question.* New York: Random House, 1978.

Miller, N. E. "The Role of Learning in Physiological Response to Stress." In *Psychopathology of Human Adaptation,* ed. George Serban. New York: Plenum Press, 1976.

Needleman, Carla. *The Work of Craft: An Inquiry Into the Nature of Crafts and Craftsmanship.* New York: Knopf, 1979.

Okun, M. A. "Adult Age and Cautiousness in Decision: A Review of the Literature." *Human Development* 19(1976):220–233.

Orwell, George. *1984.* New York: Harcourt Brace, 1949.

Ovesey, Lionel. "Fear of Vocational Success." *AMA Archives of General Psychiatry* 7(1962):82–92.

Pearlin, Leonard. "Life Strains and Psychological Distress Among Adults." In *Themes of Work and Love in Adulthood*, ed. N. J. Smelser and E. H. Erikson. Cambridge, Mass.: Harvard University Press, 1980.

Rabkin, J. G., and Struening, E. L. "Life Events, Stress and Illness." *Science* 194(3 December 1976):1013–1020.

Rahe, R. H. "The Pathway Between Subjects' Real Life Changes and Their Near-future Illness Reports: Representative Changes." In *Stressful Life Events: Their Nature and Effects*, ed. B. S. Dohrenwend and B. P. Dohrenwend. New York: Wiley, 1974.

Rust, H. L. *Jobsearch: The Complete Manual for Jobseekers*. New York: AMACOM, 1979.

Schafer, Roy. *Language and Insight*. New Haven: Yale University Press, 1978.

Selye, Hans. *The Stress of Life*. New York: McGraw-Hill, 1956.

Shapiro, David. *Neurotic Styles*. New York: Basic Books, 1965.

Spock, Benjamin. *Baby and Child Care* (new and revised 3rd ed.). New York: Hawthorn Press, 1968.

Toffler, Alvin. *Future Shock*. New York: Random House, 1970.

Tresemer, D. W. *Fear of Success*. New York: Plenum Press, 1977.

Wallach, M. A., and Kogan, Nathan. "Sex Differences and Judgment Processes." *Journal of Personality* 27(1959):555–564.

Watzlawick, Paul; Weakland, John; and Fisch, Richard. *Change: Principles of Problem Formation and Problem Resolution*. New York: Norton, 1974.

Weil, Simone. *Waiting for God*. New York: Putnam, 1951.

Weiss, J. M. "Effects of Coping Responses on Stress." *Journal of Comparative and Physiological Psychology* 65(1968):251–260.

Weiss, J. M. "Psychological Factors in Stress and Disease." *Scientific American* 226, no. 6 (1972):104–113.

Weiss, J. M.; Glazer, H. L.; Pohorecky, L. A.; Brick, J.; and Miller, N. E. "Effects of Chronic Exposure to Stressors on Avoidance-Escape Behavior and on Brain Norepinephrines." *Psychosomatic Medicine* 37(1975):522–533.

Wheeler, D. D., and Janis, I. L. *A Practical Guide for Making Decisions*. New York: Free Press, 1980.

Wheelis, Allen. *How People Change*. New York: Harper & Row, 1973.

Wheelis, Allen. *On Not Knowing How to Live*. New York: Harper & Row, 1975.

Winnicott, D. W. *Through Pediatrics to Psychoanalysis*. New York: Basic Books, 1975.

Index